Fire Girl

Fire Girl

Jan Mendoza

Library of Congress Control Number 2012931483
ISBN 9780982605042
Manufactured in the United States of America.

All events in this book did happened. However many years have passed and the author took creative license in exact timelines of certain events, dialogue and crew involved in certain instances. Names were changed and measures were taken to change physical descriptions.

www.wildlandfirewomen.com
www.janmendoza.com

Dedicated to

All Fire Girls Past, Present and Future

Foreword

"No Shit, there I was..." (the preface to any smoke jumper story). The 110 lb pack was wobbling as I leaned against a stone ledge to conserve some strength for the three mile hike. The others were still getting their packs situated. Two more of the five gals that made it thus far into rookie training came over to share the perch while we waited for the Hell Week torture to ensue. Someone with their heavy pack leaned back too far taking all three of us backwards over the edge. As we laid on our backs like helpless turtles with arms and legs flailing around, we all started laughing! Our training foreman helped us roll over and she said with a smile, "This is how it should be...you are laughing." Being a rookie was hard and there wasn't much laughing after that first day, but it was much harder and different for the first women fire fighters.

Here's to Jan (the author), to Margarita (1st grandmother smokejumper), to Deanne (1st female smokejumper) to all the 1st's and to all the rookies for years to come, thanks for following your dreams, thanks for fighting the politicians, thanks for breaking the stereotypes. This is an awesome line of work...thanks for keeping the door open!

We have this commonality but more than that we have our individuality! Every minority that has battled for equal rights is filled with people that share only one likeness yet are identified by that one characteristic. Recognizing individuality in the midst of stereotypes, generalizations, and preconceptions is the continuing battle for all including the white male.

I've known Jan only a few years. Our visits have centered around Jan's knowledge and experience trick riding, but also included some time for sharing stories of horses, kids, overseas travels and other life experiences. Getting to know her and then hearing this story paints a picture of a very resilient young girl. These characteristics still evident in her ability to demonstrate death defying stunts on the back of a running horse! Her wit in explaining to the cocky young trick riding students how it is illegal in the state of South Dakota for a person over fifty to have their butt over their head (the imaginary law she just broke) mirrors her younger personality the reader will soon come to know.

I am honored to have this space in Jan's book. I am privileged to add her story to a collection of other women. Their experiences, fights, triumphs all different and equally important are part of "America the land of opportunity" in the making. Thanks for telling your story.

Jennifer Anderson-Belitz
Firefighter/Hotshot
Smoke jumper
U.S. Fish & Wildlife Service
U.S. Forest Service
1995-2005

A Fire is Started

For the Girls

Prologue

I was a mere child of 18 years old when I took the job of seasonal firefighter with the California Department of Forestry. Since there were no other girls that I knew of doing this type of work, I didn't have any mentors and had no idea what the job would require both physically and mentally being female. I was extremely naive of the world and I didn't have much employment experience or street smarts. The voice you will hear in this story is of "that" young girl. I admit doing a little whining here and there. The day I reported to CDF, I felt like I had landed onto a foreign and sometimes hostile planet with a strange "man" language that I didn't speak. Of course now that I'm much older with more life experiences under my belt, I would have handled some of my situations differently. I also don't whine as much as I used to.

I was a seasonal fighter for only one summer. My story is a short one, but that summer taught me serious life lessons that I carried throughout adulthood and never forgot. In that short season, I not only broke a barrier (unknowingly) for women in California but I broke one for myself as well. I have huge respect and gratitude to all firefighters (especially the girls) who went back (and still go back) for more dirt, smoke and hot flames season after season.

My fire girl experience happened over 30 years ago. As some of my memories have been ingrained in my mind in fine detail for all of those 30 years, some of my memories have been purged. I imagine my brain as a big file room filled with filing cabinets. Some of these cabinets are filled to the brim and stashed way in the back collecting dust.

Since my file room stores over 50 years of crap, my brain sometimes decides to go through files, throwing out unnecessary information making room for new information. I guess my brain doesn't think that names of people are worth remembering, so out they go. So with that said, the names of most everyone in this book have been changed simply because I can't remember them.

If you are one of the people that served with me at Whitmore, you may have completely different memories than I do of this experience. Everyone's brain is organized differently and so is everyone's record retention schedule. I find it very interesting when two people who experience the same event remember it completely different. So, that's the way it goes with this book. These are my memories and if they are different from yours, I'm sorry.

When I started writing this book, I had to blow the cobwebs off some very old files in my memory vault and in order to open some of these vaults; I downloaded some of the songs that I listened to back in those days. It was amazing how listening to albums such as Todd Rundgren's "Hermit of Mink Hollow" and Black Sabbath's "Sabbath Bloody Sabbath" and Jackson Browne's "Running on Empty" opened those long locked memory vaults from that particular year. I used to blast these cassettes extremely loud in the stereo of my gold Plymouth Valiant. I find that music is very powerful in unleashing feelings and memories of a past time. Once those memories and feelings came flooding back and I became engrossed in writing them down, a few weird and very cool things happened.

Incident #1

During this journey down memory lane, I started thinking heavily about the people that were part of this time in my life. Like I said earlier, I don't remember names of most people, but I do have photos and I completely remember their personalities, their voices and the conversations that we had.

When I started writing this book, I wondered whatever became of some of the characters in my story. Then one day, out of the blue, one of these people found me on Facebook. His timing of finding me after 30 years of no contact was uncanny. He remembered some of the names that I couldn't and a few stories that I had long forgotten which helped me tremendously. He must have been receiving my telepathic messages!

Incident # 2

On one of my rare days to just sit and write, I spent hours typing away my memories of fighting my very first grass fire. I was writing in detail about how grass fires behave and how we were trained on putting them out. My deep thoughts transported me back to this time for several hours that day and I was completely engrossed in what I was writing. My husband came home from work while I was fully absorbed in my memories and thoughts. He went out onto the back porch to say hello to our dogs when I heard him yell, "There's a fire out back." I closed my laptop, in the middle of my own grass fire, only this fire was in Microsoft Word, and bolted for the door. The field just behind our property was on fire and burning at a rapid pace. Flames were high and it was really taking off, just the way I was writing about grass fires all day. Before long, a California Department of Forestry (CDF) spotter plane was buzzing the house followed by a big fire retardant tanker plane. Did this fire start because of my intense thoughts about fire? Nah… couldn't be. Weird!

And it gets even weirder…..CDF responded to a total of seven grass fires around our house during the months I was writing this book.

Incident #3

Just as I was finishing writing this book and making the final edits, I happened to be telling a co-worker about this project. He asked me if I knew a gal named Paula who used to be a CDF firefighter that worked in our building. I had no idea. Come to find out she was hired by CDF the exact same summer as me! I was ecstatic and couldn't wait to meet her.

Paula Siddons was 18 years old in 1978 when she took the CDF physical test and was assigned to the Yorba Linda CDF station in Orange County California. She was the only female and she was lucky enough to have a separate room to sleep in. In 1979, Paula went back for more and worked at the southern California desert station of Hesperia. Later that season, she was transferred to the head quarters station in San Bernardino where she worked with a female engineer. Paula said that on some shifts it was just her and the other girl alone on an engine responding to fire calls and car crashes. Paula went on to work for the California Department of Motor Vehicles where she retired from state service in 2014. I worked four floors above Paula for almost five years and never knew that we shared the same experience of being one of the first CDF female firefighters.

Strong Language Disclaimer

If the few "F" bombs or other swear words in my story offend you, I'm sorry. That's the way guys talked in this world and I wanted to give the reader the full flavor of my experience. I could have put in many more, believe me! Yes, we firefighters had potty mouths. If you get offended, just cover your eyes and move onto the next sentence.

8

ONE

A Man's World

I't's my assumption that women have been putting out fires for thousands of years. If it meant the village becoming toast, you bet the women were scurrying about beating out the flames to protect the hut. In the early days of our nation, wildland fires were fought by the townsfolk, including the women and children. It was an all-volunteer operation that knew no boundaries of gender since people were just helping neighbors and protecting their own property. As the population in the United States grew, so did the threat of wildland fires. According to the fire experts of the US government, humans were (and still are) the number one cause of wildland fires. President Benjamin Harrison figured that something should be done to protect the forests. So, with The Forest Reserve Act of 1881, he put aside 13 million acres of land for National Forests. To protect these treasured national forests, the United States Forest Service was formed and became the first organized agency to hire forest firefighters, all men of course. It wasn't until World War II, when most the menfolk went off to war, that women were hired to fight forest fires. Their service only lasted a couple of years because as soon as the war was over, the women were promptly relieved of their firefighting duties and were sent back to their homes where the only fire that was being put out was on the stove.

It seemed that women were officially allowed to do "men's work" only when there weren't any men to do the job. So, how did women finally get to be paid for fighting wildland fires? It took many years of protesting and much civil unrest; that's how. Civil rights for women were painfully slow. Here's a little known fact; African American men gained the right to vote 97 years before women of any race. Of course these men had trouble gaining access to the voting polls to exercise that right, but if they did make it to a poll, they could legally vote. Women didn't get the legal right to vote until 1920 with the passage of the 19th Amendment to the United States Constitution.

This amendment was repeatedly brought before Congress starting in 1915 and was defeated every time. Apparently, womenfolk had no business messing around with politics. I'm picturing one of those senators coming home from a hard day at the Capitol and his wife waiting at the door ready to whack him in the head with a frying pan. "Heeennry.. tell me you didn't vote no again on that women's rights law." WHACK! Makes me wonder if congressmen were showing up for work with big goose eggs on their noggins until one by one they decided to change their vote. Although women finally won the right to vote, they were still not allowed to work in many places. It took another 44 years and the enactment of the Civil Rights Act of 1964 to open the doors. This act made it illegal for any business or organization in the United States to discriminate against anyone because of their race, gender, national origin or religious beliefs. This act was an extremely important piece of legislation; however, it wasn't very strong and didn't extend to local and state government. In fact, he enforcement aspect of this law was extremely weak and it took many amendments over the next 20 years to fill in the holes. There were many gender-biased shenanigans going on in the business world and it wasn't until 1972 and a lot of jumping up and down by the lady with big aviator glasses, Gloria Steinem, leader of the Women's Liberation Movement, that the law was finally enforceable at every level of government.

There were some specific amendments in the law that paved the way for female firefighters. One in particular was an Ohio Supreme Court case that overturned the rule that said women couldn't work a job that required them to lift over 25 pounds or required them to take lunch breaks at different times than men. The United States Supreme Court also decided that printing separate job listings for men and women was illegal, which ended that practice among the country's newspapers.

Finally in 1974 the US Forest Service started hiring female wildland firefighters. They also hired the very first woman to be on a hotshot fire crew. The Forest Service hotshot crews are an elite group of highly trained firefighters that work the most remote areas of the forest for long periods of time. The Forest Service has since lost the name of this brave woman hotshot, but the Forest Service does cite the year of her hire as 1975 or 1976.

By 1974, the California Department of Conservation, Division of Forestry (CDF), as it was then called, was thinking about hiring women and started having policy meetings. One of the results of these meetings was the agreement to establish minimum performance standards, including physical requirements, to allow all applicants – men and women – to test for employment. Finally in June 1975, 11 years after the Civil Rights Act was signed, policy was made where women could finally be hired and paid for fighting wildland fires for the State of California. A memo went out to all of the CDF units that they must try to hire personnel according to the female-to-male ratio of applications received. The popular term for this system was "Affirmative Action." Even though the door was finally opened, only a couple of women applied. The next two years only saw an increase of a few more women among the several hundred men who were hired each year as seasonal firefighters. There were only 26 female seasonal firefighters (including me) working for CDF the summer of 1978. By 1988, there were over 468.* The numbers gradually grew over the years, but the ratio is still very small to this day.

Females breaking into the very dangerous job of wildland firefighting didn't come without its hurdles. Besides having to be physically able to do the work, once on the job, some women firefighters had to endure sexist remarks, chauvinism and extra pressure to perform over and beyond what was expected of men. Some women firefighters were accepted on the firelines while some were considered an annoyance, especially by their older veteran male counterparts.

We were in a man's world, but in that world we firefighting suffragettes endured, paving the way for women wildland firefighters for years to come.

Here is one fire girl's story.

---

* Statistics provided by the California State Controller and the California State Personnel Board.

TWO
Boxing Musician at a Mountain College

"**A**re you Nuts?" my dad said as I broke the news that I was going to be a seasonal forest firefighter. "Do they allow women?" 'They just started," I replied.

"Why don't you just come home for the summer and get a job at the mall or something." He wasn't doing a very good job at hiding his sarcasm as he helped me pack up my college dorm room. Little did he know, I was already hired. I started to think nervously that maybe I was a little nuts. The year was 1978.

I was never a girly girl growing up. I rode horses and loved spending my summers on my sister's cattle ranch in Alturas. When I was in elementary school, I wore cowboy boots and jeans everyday. Since my personal appearance didn't mean much to me, I refused to keep my hair combed, and my mother kept my hair in extremely tight ponytails that stuck out on each side of my head. My dad taught me how to shoot guns, fish and at 12 years old, I learned how to drive the family truck. As I grew into my teenage years and started getting an interest in boys, I eventually "girled" myself up a bit. However, I was still more interested in going to the sporting good store shopping for camping supplies and fishing tackle than shopping for clothes.

In high school, I taught myself how to snow ski, I was on the swim and gymnastics teams, and I belonged to the mountaineers backpacking club. I absolutely adored the outdoors, especially the mountains. I fantasized about riding my bicycle across the United States and spending months backpacking in the Rocky Mountains.

As a teenager, I considered myself a women's libber and started to pay attention to the women's rights movement of the 1970s. I wasn't a militant about it, but even though I never held a job myself, I did believe women should be given all of the same opportunities in the workplace as men. I hated being called a tomboy, and I never understood why certain things like fishing, hunting and sports were considered things for boys while cooking and sewing were things girls were supposed to do. I wasn't buying any of it. I was a person named Jan who could do anything and everything and don't bother to tell me otherwise!

Having sung and played guitar since the age of nine, I became a professional musician at 16, performing at weddings and at a dive bar called Dotty's in Sacramento. I had serious aspirations of being a professional musician so, when it was time for me to go off to college, it was natural for me to pick music as my major. I kind of goofed-off in high school; well actually, I goofed-off a lot which resulted in my non acceptance to a four year college. However, my parents were still willing to send me to college away from home so that I could have the dorm experience. As luck would have it, Shasta College in Redding not only had dorms, they had a decent music program. Shasta College, located in one of the most beautiful areas of California with lots of out-door recreation, was pure heaven in my book.

Redding, California is situated at the most northern edge of the massive valley that stretches for over 450 miles through the center of the state. Fairly large mountains cascade on all sides of the town with the 14 thousand foot Mt. Shasta towering just to the north and Mt. Lassen, a semi-active volcano, looming majestically to the east. The area was abundant with my favorite things: mountains, forests, many large lakes, rivers, water falls and creeks with fantastic swimming holes and fishing. Shasta College was a very picturesque school, nestled in the tall pine trees about ten miles outside of town and looked somewhat like a mountain retreat. I was in serious danger of never getting any school work done.

Days before my new college career in the fall, mom and dad dropped me and my meager belongings off at the dorms. The campus was full of kids meeting each other for the first time and dorm veterans who saw old friends after a long summer. I didn't know a soul, but I didn't care; freedom at last. I didn't own a car, but that was just fine as I had my trusty green Schwinn 10- speed that weighed 50 pounds. "The Green Tank" had been my only source of transportation for the past three years in the greater Sacramento area.

I totally loved my life in the dorms even though my first roommate was a total bitch and the room was the size of a closet. I was out of my parents' house and finally free. I got busy making lots of friends, getting invited to parties (which never happened in high school) and quickly got to know the surrounding area. As if my schedule wasn't busy enough between school and my social life, I decided to check out what collegiate sports Shasta College had to offer.

To my disappointment, Shasta College didn't have a gymnastics team, so one of my dorm friends talked me into trying out for field hockey. What the heck was field hockey? Did I need skates? The first practice was on a big grassy field - I figured skates were out. Instead, I was handed what looked like a big ice hockey stick. Only a few girls showed up for the first practice, so the coach made a quick decision to disband the team right that second. Highly disappointed, I handed back my cool new stick and headed to the dorms to search for another sport.

As I crossed the field, I spied the Shasta College cross-country track team running around the track and I headed over to watch. I was soon joined by other members of the newly disbanded girls' field hockey team which got noticed by the cross-country coach. He immediately ran over and asked us if we wanted to join the team since he was lacking girls. Hmm, running...never done that before! Most of the disbanded hockey players, including me, joined on the spot.

I soon found myself running ten miles a day along the country roads surrounding the college and traveling around the north state competing in cross-country track meets. Running cross-country was extremely hard on my legs and I started to suffer tremendously from shin splints. Shin splints hurt like living hell as the tendons were literally separating from my leg bone from the constant pounding on the asphalt. After each practice, I had to spend a lot of time with my legs soaking in buckets of ice while my coach wrapped my feet and legs like a racehorse before each meet. I tried my hardest on the team but my injuries kept me from doing well in the races.

With the upcoming summer in mind, I started to scan the campus bulletin board looking for summer jobs in the area. I couldn't see myself asking people "would you like fries with that" and being stuck working fast food like a lot of my friends, so I hoped to get a job at a retail store or working with kids at a summer camp. I would have even taken a babysitting job for the summer.

Scanning the board, I spotted an official announcement stating that the California Department of Forestry was hiring seasonal firefighters. The notice went on to say that applicants had to be in good physical condition and women and minorities were encouraged to apply. This sounded interesting but working with kids at a summer camp seemed a whole lot more fun, so I decided to wait until something more fitting was posted. After a couple of weeks of constantly checking the job board and scouring the newspaper, I was starting to get a little discouraged. I wanted to avoid going home for the summer at all costs.

Partying was a favorite past-time in the Shasta College dorms and my new roommate, Cheryl, (I had three different roommates that year) and I had a little refrigerator in our dorm room that consisted of a bottle of vodka, orange juice, graham crackers and peanut butter. Of course the "food" in the fridge was for soaking up the booze! I don't think that this was the college experience that my parents had in mind, but I was having the time of my life.

The college employed a married couple who lived in the house between the dorms to oversee us kids, but they weren't much help with my academic woes since they were the culprits who were constantly throwing big kegger dorm parties. Apparently providing alcohol to underage kids wasn't a big deal in the 70s, or so it seemed. It was at one of these big blowout parties where my destiny was about to change. Holding my favorite red party mug full of beer, I started having an intense conversation with one of my fellow dormies named Connor.

Connor was tall and lean with sandy blonde hair and wore what I considered the typical cowboy uniform; a plaid shirt and a big belt buckle. Of course, the uniform wasn't complete without the worn ring in his back pocket of his Levis made by a can of chewing tobacco. Connor was a mountain boy from Weaverville and a bit of a redneck, but I liked him and thought that he was cute. I was a sucker for cowboys.

Connor started complaining about something called CDF and how they were hiring girls. "So what's the problem?" I thought to myself as Connor continued his tirade. As his voice got louder over Journey's "Wheel in the Sky" that was blaring on the stereo, he yelled, "I can't believe they are letting girls in." OK, first off, I had no idea what CDF stood for or what he was really talking about, but his disdain for working with girls got my women's lib defensive weaponry system on full alert "What is CDF?" I asked with as much fake sympathy as I could muster. "It's the California Department of Forestry," he said. The flier on the bulletin board flashed in my mind. "I fight fires for em' in the summers and a girl better not be working at my station, I would be so pissed." Now my women's lib nuclear missile was in full launch sequence. I felt myself getting hot as I go in for the kill. "Sooo, where do I apply?"

Connor looked me up and down with a shit-eating grin on his face. "They'd never let you in. You're too puny. There's no way in hell you will pass the physical test." At this point one of his friends walked over, and Connor proceeded to tell him all about my "plans." Before I knew it, Connor's good-ole-boy buddies had gathered around and I was surrounded by plaid shirts and big buckles. As this six foot guy towered over me I craned my neck to try to look him square in the eye. "I'll not only pass the test, I'll kick your ass." Connor and his buddies rolled with laughter as I pivoted on my heel gave them the finger and stomped off.

"Crap, what did I just do? I've put my foot in it now...I'm way too drunk." My drunken mind was trying to process all of this. OK, so I liked working outside, and I loved being in the forest. I wouldn't be working with kids. How hard could this be? More drunken thoughts swarmed around. I drew the line in the sand with Connor, and I wasn't one to back down. Looking on the bright side, I thought that maybe this would be a cool and fun adventure, not to mention, I wouldn't have to spend a long and boring summer at my parents' house. I rose my beer glass, gave myself a toast, and from that moment on, I was determined to be one of those dreaded girl firefighters for the California Department of Forestry. With any luck, I would get assigned to Connor's station.

I woke up the next morning with a raging hangover, and out of my beer soaked eyes, I saw that Cheryl was getting ready for her job at Burger King. I told her the conversation with Connor and "the dare" I planned on going through with. "I can get you a job at BK- no one has died from working the drive through, that I know of," she said as she put on the final touches of her make-up. My head really hurt from too much beer and the sheer terror of what I was getting into started to settled in my stomach, or was it alcohol poisoning. I wasn't sure. I pulled the covers over my head and tried to sleep off my hangover and this nightmare - both self-induced.

The second semester of school was around the corner, and it was time to sign up for classes. I thumbed through the coarse catalog looking for music and general education classes. Like a flashing beacon, I saw "Wildland Fire Science." Bingo. I had to take this class. I had no idea what it took to be a firefighter or anything about the science of fighting fires. Here was my chance to get a head start and hopefully get an advantage over other applicants.

The course description said we would be outside a lot and to dress in work boots, jeans and a long-sleeve shirt. I had a pair of hiking boots from my back packing days that worked out just fine for class. The fire science classrooms were all the way in the back of the campus near the agriculture section called "the barns." Set apart from the rest of campus, the barns were nestled in the woods surrounded by a scattering of more portable looking buildings that served as classrooms. I noticed that there weren't many girls milling about on this side of campus, but, to my delight, I did notice that there were lots of cowboys. As I took my seat in the fire class, I nervously looked around the room and soon found that I was the only girl. This was going to be great! I was really doing it and Connor could kiss my ass. I was actually training to be a firefighter.

The instructor gave me a friendly smile which made me feel a little better. The class was more interesting than I thought it would be; actually, I didn't know what to expect. We learned all about fuel, wind, weather and how fires stay alive and how best to kill them. We marched around the campus learning how to cut into the dirt to make fire lines with shovels and hand tools that had weird names like Pulaskis, Mcleods and brush hooks. A Pulaski was a tool that was created just for firefighting in 1910 by a man named, you guessed it, Pulaski. This odd looking tool had an axe blade on one side and directly opposite the axe blade there was a hoe-type tool for digging in the dirt. The Mcleod, that was invented by a guy named, (here we go again) Mcleod had a rake on one side and a flat blade type of tool on the other side for scraping and clearing the ground. The brush hook (a hook shaped axe looking gadget) was a tool that was swung onto brush limbs, slicing them off with one or two strokes. Using these crazy tools, we manually scraped and dug all vegetation away and made dirt trails. The tools were heavy, and I did a lot of grunting and groaning as I swung them with all of my might to try and make a dent on the foliage. These dirt trails, called fire lines, helped keep the fire from spreading, or so they told us. We were told that if you take away the fuel, such as dried grass, wood, leaves, etc., the fire would slow its rate of spread, since dirt doesn't burn. The dinky little dirt trails that we cut in the woods behind the college sure didn't look like much, and I couldn't imagine that these little three-foot-wide paths would stop a raging fire. But, what did I know? I kept digging, grunting and sweating.

The students in my class were a mixture of guys wanting to be career firemen and seasonal firefighters like me. As the class progressed, I made a few friends and learned some of the ins and outs of getting a seasonal firefighting job with CDF. Everyone in the class was, for the most part, friendly and encouraging, but I didn't think any of them took me seriously or thought that I'd really be hired. As I learned the fundamentals of being a firefighter in the classroom, I knew I'd have to step up my game if I was going to pass the physical test. My classmates were a wealth of information regarding the testing requirements of CDF.

I would have to run a mile with 45 pounds of hose on my back, do 50 sit-ups with a 10-pound weight behind my head in less than a minute, and perform a step test to see if my heart rate was up to par. I figured that I would have to curtail my drinking and partying and start some serious training. Time was running out and I had to get in the best shape of my life.

At the beginning of spring semester, a new girl moved into the dorm room directly across the hall from me. Lauren was strikingly beautiful with her very long sun-bleached hair, piercing blue eyes and she wore cute sun dresses that showed off her perfectly tanned legs. The moment I met her I knew this girl was light years different from the other girls in the dorms who were all from Hicksville, USA. Lauren was from Los Angeles, listened to hard rock music, was adventurous and we soon became best friends. Lauren and I were inseparable, and we ran all over town in her orange Datsun station wagon – hanging out at the lake and doing everything except study. While Lauren and I were walking out of the cafeteria one spring day, we passed by a table that peaked our interest. The Shasta College boxing club was looking for members. "How are you girls doing?" asked a very nice looking and extremely buff black man. "You want to learn to box?" Lauren and I looked at each other and said collectively, "OK!"

The next day, our instructor Keith outfitted with us with ridiculously huge boxing gloves. We proceeded to train with an intensity that I had never felt in my life. Training as a boxer was more strenuous than all of the sports I had ever experienced combined. Lauren and I spent hours jumping rope, hitting huge boxing bags and sparring. Standing at a boxing bag and punching it for three minutes straight with five pound gloves on your hands was a lot harder than it looked especially with skinny, bony arms like mine. Keith would hold the bag and a stop watch and it felt as if my arms would burst into flames before he told me I could stop when the three minutes were up. We worked out almost every day in the boxing club and Keith turned us into bad-ass fighting athletic machines. I ran seven miles a day, competed with the cross-country team and boxed. My focus was to get hired with CDF, and since my other college courses were taking a backseat, it wasn't long until I was on academic probation. I was on a mission to get hired by CDF, and I didn't really care about anything else. School was coming to an end. As the weather warmed up, Lauren and I spent most days at the lake or sunbathing on the roof of the college dorms. It was getting really hard to get to classes since I was taking advantage of the good weather to go on my training runs around the campus. I was easily able to do 100 sit-ups with 20-pound weight in a very fast time. When I wasn't running and jumping rope, I was punching that big boxing bag with my boxing coach.

It had been a month since I sent in my application to CDF, and I anxiously waited for a reply. In the meantime my life was all about training, training and more training.

"You got a letter from CDF today," said Cheryl. Exhausted from my boxing training I just sat on my bed staring at the letter afraid to touch it. "Are you gonna open it?" Cheryl yelled. "Screw it; I'll open it for you." She leaped for the envelope and landed back on her bed with a thud. Just as she was pulling the letter out of the envelope, I snatched it from her hands.

On official California Department of Conservation, Department of Forestry letterhead I was duly informed that I had been selected to proceed to the physical testing phase of the application process of seasonal firefighter. The physical test was in one week.

My beloved firefighting Redwings that
I've kept since 1978

THREE
New Boots & Boot Camp

O n the day of the physical test at a local high school in Redding, I was very nervous and was barely able to eat breakfast. I pulled into the parking lot and saw a line of men waiting to get in. I was so nervous and I fought to keep from puking up my oatmeal. I could have easily turned around, headed back to the dorms and scrapped this whole idea. However, the image of that jerk Connor with his shit-eating grin was engrained in my head. I parked my car and took my place in the line of guys who were all wearing gym clothes. Looking up and down the long line, I didn't see one girl. You have got to be kidding me! I couldn't believe this, I was the only girl? OK, there had to be some girls already inside. However, the way I was getting gawked at, I was starting to think otherwise. Women were encouraged to apply, so why didn't they? When it was my turn at the check-in table, I was handed a questionnaire that asked about illnesses, heart problems and if I was pregnant. I laughed because I thought this last question had to be new!

The gymnasium buzzed with about 200 men doing sit-ups while some were stepping up and down on stairs. I made my way to the sit-up testing area where about 20 guys were busy doing sit-ups while the next person in line held down a pair of feet. It was my turn to hold down a pair of feet for a chubby boy who feverishly strained at his sit-ups.

"Ooonnne, twoooo, thhrreee…you better kick it up man," said the official to the red faced kid.

"Dang, you didn't practice did you?" I said to him as I held down his feet with my knees.

"Fouuurrre, Fiiive, ok, that's it man, you're done," said the official. "OK ma'am your turn, down on the mat."

As the chubby kid rolled off the mat and shuffled away, I took my position. With my legs bent and the next guy in line holding my feet, I took the ten pound weight and put it behind my head. I heard "GO" and I took off like a bullet. After training with a 20 pound weight, the 10-pound weight felt like a feather and I did the required 50 sit-ups in half the time allowed. "Good job," said the official, "Now head over for the step test."

The step test consisted of running up and down three steps as fast as I could in three minutes. This test measured my cardiovascular fitness based on how quickly my heart rate returned to normal after I was done. "OK go," said the official. I ran up and down the steps in the allotted time barely out of breath. As the official took my pulse, he said that I just might have had the best score so far! All that jump rope and running paid off.

I felt pretty confident about passing my CDF tests until I was about to do my third physical challenge, the run. As we assembled outside at the running track, I saw a huge pile of packs and rolled up fire hose. I was a little scared of this test since I hadn't practiced my runs with weight on my back. One of the officials waved me over to the big pile and handed me a green military rucksack that looked like it was left over from WWII. As I struggled to get the worn out cotton straps over my shoulders I immediately knew I was in trouble. This big ugly pack was extremely uncomfortable and when he filled it up with fire hose, the weight of it really hurt my shoulders and back. There was no way I was going to be able to run with this crazy pack digging into my shoulders for the entire way. I settled my load as best as I could and took my place on the starting line.

The pack was almost as big as me and if I were to fall over, I'd be like a stuck turtle. "Go," the official yelled and I took off running. My feet and legs felt extremely heavy and the backpack flopped on my back hard as I made my way around the first lap. I didn't run my fastest, but I ran consistent. I had to at least finish this race. "Just keep going, run, run, run," I said to myself over and over. With two laps down, my shoulders hurt so bad and I had my doubts about making it. "Run, run, run" over and over in my head. I must have sounded like a lunatic as I started to say run, run, run out loud, but it kept my mind off of the pain and my unbalanced load. I wasn't paying any attention to where the others were in this torture race; I just ran.

As I came around the final turn, my shoulders felt like they were dislocated because it hurt so badly, and the skin on the front of my shoulders were rubbed raw through my t-shirt. I finally hit the finish line and threw the pack to the ground feeling completely defeated. My fire career was over, I just knew it. I ran so slow there was no way I passed. "Congratulations," the official said. "You barely made it with 30 seconds to spare." Are you kidding me? I made it? Wiping the sweat out of my eyes and in serious pain, I limped my way back into the building. Now it was time for the "interview." I was told to go have a seat and my name would be called in a few minutes. The hallway was full of chatter as the other applicants compared their times and test scores. I sat staring at the wall in silence, chewing what fingernails I had left -not making eye contact with anyone. One by one, names were called as nervous prospects took turns to be grilled in the interview room. After about ten minutes, a prospect emerged from his interrogation showing no signs of victory or defeat.

I wish someone would have given me a clue as to what to expect. I got nothing as they emerged one after the other. I felt queasy. "Cornett." I stopped breathing and looked up to see a man in a uniform looking up and down the hallway of waiting victims.

I stood up with shaky knees, either from the brutal run or nerves, or a combo of both and made my way to the open door. Inside the interview room sat three CDF officials who sat silently behind a long table. Each man wore green pants, a khaki shirt, name tag and CDF patches on their sleeves. They looked highly official and the uniforms were a little intimidating. None of them smiled and one of them, who had a big mustache, didn't look up at all as I took a seat in the lonely chair in front of them. If the step test didn't get my heart pumping, sitting in this "hot seat" sure enough did.

"Jan Cornett, our only female," said the official with the mustache. "Did you know that you held the step test record today? You're in darned good shape." he said with his eyes fixed on a piece of paper. "Yes, I nervously reply, I'm on the Shasta College cross-country team."

"Well as you probably know, there are only a couple of women working for CDF and you were the only one to test here today." I stared blankly back at them as they thumbed through my application. They asked me all sorts of questions about school and seemed impressed that I had already taken the wildland fire class.

They also told me that I needed to cut my hair shorter. Ok, hold the phone! My Dorothy Hamill haircut was already very short-what were they talking about? I just nodded in agreement. "Welcome aboard! You will start your fire training in one week."

The salary was $550-a-month for five 24-hour shifts a week, room and board included. Sounded like deal to me, especially the room and board part. I was handed a packet containing a list of things that I needed to buy and each of the CDF officials shook my hand as I got up to leave. I walked out of the interrogation room with a huge smile, forgetting about my physical pain and raw shoulders. Mission number one of passing the test was over. Mission number two was to head back to the boys dorm and rub mission number one in Connor's face, I was hired!

One thing that I learned in my firefighting class was that a good pair of wildland firefighting boots were worth their weight in gold. With the miles of hiking and trudging through the woods, a good pair of boots would save your life. I heard that Redwings were the boots of choice and since boots were first on my equipment list, I happily went and did my favorite thing, shopping. I looked at the price tag on the Redwings in disbelief. Eighty dollars was a lot of money to a starving college student that lived on graham crackers and peanut butter. The boots I chose were a thing of beauty. They laced up high above my ankles and smelled of new leather. I loved my boots and I wore them everywhere to break them in before fire season. I tried to get them as dirty as possible so I wouldn't look like such a greenhorn my first day at work, as if that would have made a difference.

I went to the suggested uniform store and bought work gloves, the same dark green uniform slacks and short and long-sleeve khaki shirts that the officials wore in my interview and CDF patches.

A bandana was also on the list. I figured the bandana was to go on my head so I bought a pretty blue one. I couldn't wait to get my new CDF uniforms back to the dorms and get busy sewing my official CDF patches on my brand new shirts. I was officially a firefighter.

When my parents came up to Redding to move my things out of the dorms for the summer, I broke the news to them that I wasn't coming home. My dad thought that I had completely lost my mind, and my mother was worried beyond belief. "I'm already hired and I start fire training next week," I announced. As they were leaving, my mother gave me a hug and told me not to get myself killed. She knew forest fires very well since she grew up in the forests of Northern California. She saw a fire almost overtake her child hood home as her father and neighbors fought feverishly to beat the raging forest fire that took out most of the town. When I finished with my finals, I was able to stay in the dorms for one more week which worked out great since I had fire training and wouldn't be officially assigned to a fire station until my training was finished.

The day finally arrived for my first day of fire training and once again I couldn't eat my breakfast. My appetite had a habit of making itself scarce when I was nervous, and since I was only 95 pounds, I couldn't afford not to eat so I choked down my staple, graham crackers with peanut butter. After I put on my newly acquired CDF get-up, complete with my hand-sewn patches, I took a look at myself in the mirror. I looked damned sharp from head to toe, even with my new "butch" haircut. Oh no, my boots weren't dirty enough! I had to make sure and get more dirt on them before I was seen.

The main CDF fire station in Redding was good sized with several garages that held fire trucks and other forest type of pickups and vehicles. There was a mass of guys all dressed like me milling about near the garages. Some of their boots looked brand new but not mine! Not knowing where to go, I headed over to a group of guys who looked as lost as I did. At 8:00 a.m. sharp, we lined up outside one of the garages and signed in. We were handed hard hat helmets, fire-resistant suits called Nomex® and goofy looking clear plastic safety goggles. I swore that these were the same goggles that kids used in woodshop. Upon closer inspection, these flimsy goggles sure didn't seem like they would be very effective.

After I collected all of my gear, I was handed a piece of paper with a number. "If you are holding numbers one through five, gather over by that garage door," yelled an older man who I assumed was a boss.

I soon found out that the boss pecking order goes like this: Seasonal firefighters, such as myself, worked only during fire season on a temporary basis for a minuscule wage. The apparatus engineer, was the crew leader and authorized to drive the fire truck and the captain, who was also a full-time employee, was the head of the entire fire station. There were also Battalion Chiefs who oversaw a group of fire stations, but I didn't have personal dealings with these people. In order to work your way through the ranks, firefighters had to work a few seasons and test for the full-time / year-round positions.

"Wow, a girl!" All eyes turned to me as I stood at least a foot shorter than the rest of the group which was very noticeable. "Heard we might have a girl here this year," said a tall lanky guy who immediately made it known to the group that this was his third season. As we introduced ourselves, we were told to file into a classroom where we would learn all about fire. I was surprised to see the same instructor that I had back at Shasta College and he taught an exact re-run of what I had learned the past semester. We did classroom work for a few days then on the 4th day we were told to suit up in our Nomex and meet out by the garages. I watched as the three-year veteran swiftly got into the front passenger seat of one of the fire trucks; the rest of us were directed to sit on the little benches on the back of the truck.

The CDF fire trucks were compact and meant for fighting wildland fires. They held 500 gallons of water, had a fire pump and various sizes of hoses. The trucks were red with rotating emergency beacons on top and had a siren. The trucks were also outfitted with all of the hand tools that I practiced with in my firefighting class as well as canteens of water, breathing apparatuses (MSA) and other equipment. The back of the truck was open air with a roll bar and had two bench seats that faced each other. Firefighters rode in these back jump seats, strapped in and exposed to the elements.

I took my seat in the back for the very first time and struggled with my seat belt, my helmet and my bulky woodshop goggles. I still found it hard to believe that I was really doing this and was actually sitting on a real fire truck. I never thought of being a firefighter in my entire life, and here I was being one.

As we cruised through town, people on the street and in cars took notice of us. I wondered if they thought that there was a child or one of the firemen's daughters sitting with the crew in the back. I was getting many looks from motorists and soon enjoyed the attention and gave a small nod or wave to people as we passed by. Our convoy came to a stop near a grassy field just outside of town that was soon set ablaze. This was our training fire. It was the only fire that I got to practice on before fighting the real thing. We scrambled off the trucks and were given a quick lesson on how to operate the 300 gallon-per-minute pump that brought the water through the hoses.

We learned how to take the hose fittings on and off and how to connect hoses to to make longer hoses. We also learned how to hold the hose as a team and how to be completely ready when the pump operator started sending water through it. If you weren't hanging onto the hose properly, you could be in for a wild ride as the pressure from the water would send that hose flying in all directions like a wild snake – making it nearly impossible to get a hold of again. When the bosses felt we were ready and knowledgeable on the basic operation of the truck and how to manipulate the hose and nozzle, the field was methodically set on fire and we practiced putting it out.

Trying to put out a grass fire was like trying to herd cats that were running in all directions at lightning speed. Just when we were getting a handle on one side of the fire the wind shifted and with a flash, the fire moved in the other direction in the dead dry grass. Grass fires could take out entire neighborhoods in minutes if there was a strong wind.

My first experience with a grass fire happened when I was a kid. My visiting cousin accidentally set the field on fire behind our house while playing with matches. We watched that fire take off like a rocket as my dad scrambled in futility trying to put it out with the garden hose. It was all very exciting, but my cousin got in a world of trouble.

There were different size hoses on the truck with the biggest hose being 1 1/2 inches in diameter and made of cotton. These bigger hoses could put out a lot of water very fast. There was also a smaller hose on a reel called a booster hose. This hose was just a tad larger than a garden hose at 3/4 inches in diameter. The booster hose was used to mop-up hot spots, smoldering embers and other smaller fires where not much water was needed.

We used the "big" hose on this practice fire. "CORNETT," yelled the engineer over the loud pump and the roar of the fire. "Get hold of that hose, right behind Miller, and help him take it around that way." As he was barking orders at me, I tried to remember what I learned in the classroom. What was all that drawing the instructor did on the chalk board? Crap, I couldn't remember! I ran out and grabbed hold of the hose just as the engineer let loose with the water at the pump. The hose instantly inflated in my gloved hands and it didn't seem that I was doing much to hold it. All I could do was try and not drop it to the ground (that would have been very bad) and helped pull it around for Miller who was controlling the nozzle. We got around to where the fire seemed to be heading and tried to stop it from going any further. The grass was high and almost to my knees. The fire was hot and spreading fast. Experienced firemen stood by watching the show as us greenhorns ran around like idiots trying to wrangle our hose and get ahead of this crazy wildfire. The pros were ready to take over if the fire got away from us, which I thought was inevitable at this point.

When it was my turn to work the nozzle of the hose I was surprised that it was somewhat heavy. As soon as I opened the nozzle for the first time I was jerked back with force and I had to keep my legs spread in a lunge stance with one foot out forward of my body to keep from being pushed backwards. It took every muscle I had on my five-foot frame to control the hose and direct the stream where I wanted it to go.

Being so close to the fire with the nozzle, I got my first experience of the intense heat and smoke that was associated with fire. If you've ever sat next to a camp fire when the wind shifted and you briefly got some thick smoke and heat in your face, your eyes would sting and tear up for a minute until you could move your chair around to the other side of the fire and away from the smoke. I didn't get the option to move out of the smoke because it was everywhere. My eyes badly watered and I couldn't see a damned thing through my cheap plastic goggles. My nose burned like I had just stuck a lit match up my nostril. The other firefighters soaked their bandanas with water and put them over their faces. Ahh. I finally understood why this was on my shopping list! I pulled out my pretty blue bandana and tied it over my nose and mouth. This helped me somewhat from choking on the smoke but I still found myself holding my breath a lot.

When we were done practicing with the hose we were introduced to the "back pump." These large bulky metal canisters of water were pure torture to carry. We loaded them on our backs and manually squirted water from a tiny hose that was attached. Armed with our back pumps, we moved to the front of the grass fire and squirted water. "They can't been be serious with these things," I thought to myself as I was feverishly pumping and squirting this tiny stream of water onto the burning grass with flames racing towards me. I really didn't like this awful device and it painfully cut into my back.

We spent most of the day putting out the grass fire and soaking the field with water so that not one inch of it was left with a burning ember. As I climbed back onto the truck, my once bright yellow Nomex suit had a gray tinge to it and my boots were covered in ash and soot. After today we were ready to be real firefighters, or so we thought.

Whitmore Fire Station circa 1978
Barracks on right - dining hall on left

FOUR
Whitmore

Back at the Shasta College dorms, a party was thrown to celebrate the end of the school year. I had decided that I wasn't going back to school the next year so I said goodbye to some of my fellow dormies forever as I figured I'd probably never see them again. I wasn't college material at that particular time and I really didn't know what I wanted to do with my life. All I knew was that I was a firefighter at the moment and that I was about to embark on a huge adventure. My friends thought that I was crazy and gave me a lot of ribbing.

"It was pretty intense out there," I said.

"Wait till you get on a big one, then you're gonna feel some heat," Connor said with a concerned look. "Well, here's to not getting killed," I said as I raised my beer. We toasted and that was the last I ever saw of Connor, the guy who dared me to be a firefighter.

The next morning, my last day as a trainee, I reported back to the CDF training center in Redding. We were about to find out where in Northern California we would be assigned. As last names were called, we were handed a piece of paper with the name of our assigned station. My paper said Whitmore with directions on how to get there.

I had never heard of this place and the map of squiggly long country roads made it seem that I would be driving off into oblivion. We were grouped together according to our stations and I got to meet my five permanent crew members that I would be working and living with for the summer. Of course I was the only girl.

The guys were all between the ages of 18 and 20ish and most of them had worked prior seasons. Mathers, who had worked the previous season, seemed to be somewhat of a jock. He was friendly and had a great sense of humor. Compton, who had worked prior seasons as well, didn't seem so friendly to me. This guy had a mischievous look about him and a scowl on his face that looked as if he just smelled something bad – I could tell right away that he wasn't exactly thrilled that there was a girl in the group. There was also Gomez and Brooks and both seemed easy going and nice enough.

Then there was Stackmore. He was pudgy kid who seemed a little odd and quirky. Stackmore didn't say much and stood there shuffling awkwardly from one foot to the other. As I sized-up my crew mates I knew I was going to have my work cut out for me winning the trust of these guys. We all shook hands and were sent off to get our certificates of completion for the 40 hours of fire training, plus instructions on when and how to report to our stations Monday morning.

I spent my last weekend as a "civilian" with my parents and my dad riddled me with never-ending questions about my new life as a firefighter. "Where are you going to sleep?" "Do you get your own room?" "What about the bathroom?" My dad went on and on with his concerns and questions for which I had no answers. As I fell asleep on my last night in a room of my own, I asked the same questions.

Studying my map, I surmised that Whitmore was a tiny town - a speck on the map about 50 miles due east of Redding, towards Mt. Lassen. The drive from Redding was windy, and it took me about an hour to get there. The little community of Whitmore consisted of a few homes nestled in the forest, a grocery store, a post office and not much else. Finding the big sign that said "Whitmore CDF Station," I pulled my 1969 gold Plymouth Valiant into the parking lot next to a shiny maroon pick-up.

The station was located in a grove of ponderosa pines with several buildings- all painted green- which made them camouflaged within the forest. There was a small office at the entrance of the station, two other long buildings and at the far end, was the garage that housed three fire trucks. On the outskirts of the station and nestled in the trees was a private looking residence painted the same color as the rest of the buildings. I got out of my car, and with gear in hand, I walked across the wide gravel driveway.

The fire radio crackled to life on the station loudspeaker that resonated throughout the surrounding forest. "Redding-Southfork" said a woman with a southern drawl. "I have smoke at 30 degrees north-45 degrees. Then a man's voice responded, "Southfork-Redding, 10-4." Seconds later, a series of tones sounded over the speaker followed by the man's voice reciting some numbers and something about a fire north of Redding.

The chatter over the loudspeaker with these crazy tones was a foreign language to me. Lugging my gear bag, I walked into the little office where there was an older looking man sitting at a small metal desk talking on the phone. He waved me over to a chair and as he continued his phone conversation, I took this opportunity to look at my surroundings. Hanging from the walls of this very old and dingy office were maps of the area. Sitting in the corner of the office was another fire radio crackling with static.

He finally hung up, looked at me long and hard, and I could tell by the way he was pursing his lips, didn't much like what he saw. "I heard I was getting one of you girls, I was hoping for a bigger one," he said with a chuckle. "I'm Jan Cornett." I reached out my hand. He grabbed it, squeezing tight around my tiny bony fingers and introduced himself as Captain Harris. I smiled trying not to grimace from the pain. "Well come on, lets get you settled," he said as he got up and headed for the door. As we walked across the drive to the barracks, I spotted Mathers and I was relieved to see a familiar face.

The barracks looked just like what I had seen in old Army movies with small beds all lined up in a row, four on each side, topped with green blankets. I knew I wasn't going to get my own room when I signed up, but it didn't really hit me until I saw the line of beds for the first time. I was really going to be sleeping with these guys. Just past the row of beds were the closets. Compton was busy putting his gear away in a closet and never acknowledged our presence. Mathers pointed to an empty bed at the end of one of the rows next to the closets, and I was thankful that I didn't have someone sleeping on both sides of me.

Mathers, the seasoned veteran, showed me how to put away my gear so that I could easily get to it if we got called out on a fire in the middle of the night. Boots and socks were kept right next to our beds with our Nomex suits, gloves, and other articles of clothing kept in neat order in our closets for easy access in the dark. "OK

Cornett, get settled, Mathers will show you the rest of the place," said Captain Harris.

Mathers took me down the adjoining hall and showed me the one and only bathroom with three shower stalls that I had to share with the rest of them. "This is going to get interesting," I said. "Yeah, we'll have to figure out a schedule," Mathers laughed. I was warned to wear my rubber thongs at all times while in the bathroom because of something called athlete's foot and other fungi I could catch. I hadn't heard of such things before and was a little taken back.

By this time, all the staff had arrived and a meeting was called in the dining building. Captain Harris introduced us to our supervisor Engineers Singer and Abbott. Singer reminded me of a marine drill sergeant and his de meaner intimidated me. Abbott was younger and seemed pretty easy going with a friendly smile. Harris gave us the rundown of the routine at Whitmore and we were told that there was to be no drinking, no drugs and no girls in the barracks. That last item got a chuckle out of everyone as they all turned and looked at me. "You guys know what I mean," said the captain raising one eyebrow at the rest of the crew. Visitors were not allowed until after 5:00 p.m. and not without prior approval. We were told that each of us would have to take turns cooking the daily meals. This had me worried since I really didn't know how to cook. Harris gave us our work schedules and my days off were Mondays and Tuesdays. We were not allowed to leave the barracks during the five days we were working, not even after 5:00 p.m. Everyone was expected to do chores around the station during the day when we weren't working a fire.

At the end of our orientation we were finally given our truck assignment, and mine was truck number 2475. "OK, now get to work," said the Captain. And with that, he stood up and marched back over to his little office. "OK, you heard him, we'll get started with a short lesson on tool sharpening," said "Sergeant" Singer as he waved us out of the dining room door.

Singer walked with a quick pace over to a small shed that was filled with hand tools, shovels, Polaskis, Mcleods and the rest of the tools that I learned to use at Shasta College. We didn't have chain saws at the fire station and didn't carry any on the trucks. We only had the use of hand tools. I guess there were insurance and liability issues; I wasn't sure. We all grabbed a tool and Singer proceeded to show us how to sharpen these tools using a big metal file.

Sitting on a log, I placed the shovel handle between my legs with the head of the shovel resting on my knees. Singer showed us how to get the blades just right with the file, turning the tool over and working both sides. There was something therapeutic about sharpening the tools, and I started to get into a rhythm as I filed away. We spent the rest of the afternoon sharpening hand tools and getting acquainted with our assigned trucks. My truck, 2475, was exactly like the truck I got to ride in during my training. There were jump seats in the back with two of the dreaded back pumps held in slots directly in the back of the truck. We were shown where the oxygen tanks and the first aid kit were kept as well as our many canteens of water. The trucks were really quite simple, and other than the pump for the water, there really wasn't much to them. I also learned what all of those tones meant that I kept hearing on the station loud speaker. The tones were set off by a dispatcher in Redding on a device called a Plectron. Each fire station was assigned its own series of high and low tones, and after each set of tones, the dispatcher called out station names and truck numbers followed by directions to an incident which could be a fire or a car wreck. We could hear fire stations from our area and surrounding counties called out to fires or other incidents. Some days, the radio would be very quiet with no tones at all. On other days, the radio would be singing with tones all day long. The tone for Whitmore was very distinct and we got to know it quickly.

My first day as a firefighter at Whitmore ended with a big dinner served in the dining room. Since it was our first night and we hadn't split up the meal duties yet, our first meal was cooked by the captain's wife Marge Harris who was very sweet to us. Mrs. Harris was very pleased to see a girl in fire camp and told me that she found it refreshing since she had been the only female for years. As she was whipping up steaks, salad and French bread, she told us stories of fire seasons past with all of the crews that had come and gone in her years at Whitmore.

As the crew ate and got to know one another better, suddenly tones started to sound on the loud speaker. Since I didn't know the tones yet, I didn't give it much thought as I had been hearing these tones all day. Mathers shot up out of his seat and headed out into the yard. After the tones, the dispatcher called two truck numbers 2480 and 2475. "Holy shit, that's my truck." We all scrambled out of the dinning room and headed for the garages. I was a nervous wreck as I fumbled with my Nomex pants, having a heck of a time getting them on over my boots. My first day at Whitmore and I was already being called out.

I should have practiced more of getting on my suit in an emergency! During all of the commotion of getting on my gear and myself onto the truck, I didn't hear what we were going to. I just assumed it was a fire. I made a last minute check that everything was on and in place; gloves, helmet, goggles, scarf and Nomex. I looked over at Gomez who seemed calm and collected as we headed down the road with the siren blaring. "Is it a fire?" I asked. "It's a logging truck roll-over and the driver was thrown out," said Gomez.

I wondered what we would do when we got there. None of us were taught first aid or CPR! We were shown where the first aid kit was kept on the truck, but we weren't shown how to use any of the contents. Unless there was a fire to put out on or near the wrecked truck, I really had no idea what we would do once we got to the scene.

As we raced down the winding mountain road, my mind started to go crazy with images of blood and guts and how I would react to seeing that. Would I get sick? Would I pass out? Would it make me cry? I was scared out of my mind and wondered if I would see a dead guy squished under a pile of logs or in pieces from being rolled on by his truck.

As our truck slowed down, I got my first glimpse of the carnage in the road. Logs were scattered everywhere and a big truck was upside-down and hanging partially over an embankment. We all piled out of the truck and walked over to the cab. There were a few motorists and other personnel at the scene but there wasn't anything anyone could do. The driver was dead and crushed in the mangled cab. I got a glimpse of his twisted legs and didn't want to see any more. I never saw a dead person before and my first day as a firefighter wasn't going to be my first time.

Nope, I wasn't seeing blood and guts that day, no way. I stood next to our truck as the rest of the guys gazed at the dead man. Since the Highway Patrol was on scene and there was no threat of fire we loaded back onto the truck.

Dusk was upon us we rambled leisurely along the mountain road heading back to the station. As I recovered from my shock, I took in the beauty of the trees and the sweet smell of the pines in the warm evening summer air. I couldn't help but think about that poor truck driver who wouldn't be making it home for dinner, and he would never smell the pines or see these trees again. This was my first experience of the meaning of life and death in the mountains of Northern California.

Whitmore CDF crew center

Driver dies in crash

(R-S photo by Gary Miller)

Crews work to remove Lewis Kelley, 61, of Burney after his log truck overturned about 4:45 p.m. Friday on Whitmore Road, just east of Cow Creek Road. Kelley died before rescue workers were able to remove him from the cab, which was crushed when the truck went off the edge of the road and rolled over. Special extraction equipment was dispatched from The Redding Fire Department, and volunteer crews were on hand from Millville a n d Whitmore fire departments. T h e California Department of Forestry a n d Mercy Medical Center personnel also responded.

The back of the fire truck where the crew sat
Notice the metal back pumps underneath.
Circa 1978

FIVE
Sweeping Mopping Mowing
Where's the Fire?

Sleeping in a room full of snoring, farting men had its challenges. Wake up call was at 6:00 a.m. and as we dragged our tired bodies out of our beds and to the shower, I learned very quickly that I needed to get in the shower first or I would be late for breakfast. There were more of them than me. All dressed and ready to go, we walked in the cool morning mountain air to the dining room where breakfast was being prepared by the crew member whose turn it was to cook. Breakfast was a big affair complete with pancakes, eggs, bacon, sausage, omelets and toast and it smelled great.

While we ate breakfast, Singer came in and gave us a weather briefing. The forecast called for hot temperatures in the mid 90s to low 100s, low humidity and a slight chance of thunderstorms in the afternoon in the higher elevations. This was perfect weather for fire and California had been in a devastating drought for the past few years. I hoped we would get a call. After breakfast we pulled the trucks out of the garages and got them ready for the day. The two way radio was checked and we fired up the pumps to make sure everything was working. The oxygen tanks were inspected and the canteens had to be dumped out and refilled with fresh drinking water from the garden hose then placed back onto the trucks. When we were finished with the truck inspections, we proceeded to do "busy work." This was the stuff that filled up our eight-hour day so that the State of California tax payers could get their money's worth out of us when we weren't fighting fires. That meant we had to find things to do or the captain or engineer would find things for us. Basically, the "other duties as required" statement in the job description meant we were grounds keepers, truck washers, cooks, janitors and mechanics.

After the trucks were ready to go, Singer told me to sweep the grounds; my first busy work assignment. Taking the big push broom, I looked at "the grounds" and all I saw was gravel and grass. What exactly was I supposed to sweep? As I stood there looking perplexed, Singer pointed to the cement gutters and paths that lined the massive grassy yards that were completely covered in pine needles. "Make them clean," he said. I made my way around the station sweeping pine needles out of the seemingly endless line of cement gutters. I felt like I had accomplished a great deal until I turned to admire my work and found that pine needles had already fallen where I swept. I looked up at the 100 foot ponderosa pines towering over my head. Dang these trees were tall. Every few seconds a breeze would whistle through the skyscraper sized pine trees making it rain pine needles.

Knowing this was a complete waste of time, I figured I'd make a day of it so I wouldn't be assigned to something even more boring. So, in the 100 degree heat, I swept for the next four hours until lunch, then after lunch, I swept for another four hours until dinner. After a full day of sweeping, it didn't look like I had done a thing all day as pine needles once again blanketed the station.

I had survived my first week at Whitmore and the days were long and tedious with lots of busy work. When the Plectron sounded over the loud speaker, we got all excited at the prospect of leaving the station and were extremely disappointed when it was another station that was called.

I was getting to know the personalities of my co-workers and I made the decision that Stackmore was a complete "wing nut" who didn't seem to understand the simplest instructions. He had to be told at least three times before he "got it." I wondered how Stackmore would perform under pressure during a real fire call. It was a mystery to me how he passed his interview and got hired for this job. I got along pretty well with the rest of the guys, except Compton. He was constantly giving me a hard time. If he was trying to make me tough, it was working! He was a constant thorn. However, the incompetent and weird Stackmore was the one that worried me. Was he going to have my back on a fire? As much as Compton irritated me, I knew he was an experienced firefighter and would know what to do if things got crazy. Stackmore...not so much.   I   t was another very hot day at Whitmore, and I was back to sweeping pine needles. Some of the other guys were clearing the small scrub brush nearby and I heard one of them yell out "hey Cornett, go over there and chop down that tree," I looked to see Compton with his usual smirk pointing to pine tree that looked to be about eight or ten feet tall.   I   hesitantly walked over and grabbed an axe. I had sharpened the axes, but I had never used one. It was heavy in my hand and I knew it was extremely sharp because one thing I got good at quickly was tool sharpening.

With one wrong swing, I could have easily chopped my leg or foot or worse, lose my grip and send the axe flying – cutting someone else in two. I was shaking when I walked up to the tree and took my first swing with everything I had. The blade of the axe bounced off of the tree like I had hit cement. I heard the group giggle.

With my face flushed with embarrassment, I took another swing. This time my axe got stuck in the tree and I couldn't get it back out! The giggling turned in to full blown laughter. Knowing that it would take me forever to chop down this tree and that I'd be the entertainment for the day, I stopped the show.

"I'm not chopping down a perfectly healthy tree just for your enjoyment," I said.

"Yeah, I figured you'd wimp out," said Compton.

By now Mathers and Gomez arrived and saw me and my nemesis Compton in a standoff.

"The little girl can't chop down that tree," said Compton.

"There is nothing wrong with this tree," I said.

"Come on, Singer wants us in the garage," said Mathers. As we walked across the yard, Mathers whispered to me that he'd give me axe swinging lessons later. Yep, Mathers and I were going to be great friends. I eventually got good at swinging an axe but not without taking a few nicks off of my boots during my learning curve.

At the garage, Engineer Singer was waiting for us with rags and cans of solvent. Singer was very hard nosed and acted just like the Marine drill sergeant that I thought he looked like. He wasn't very personable and had no sense of humor whatsoever. When it came to making up busy work for us, he was a master. All lined up in the garage, we waited with baited breath to see what assignment he had come up with this time. "Get some coveralls on and get to scraping," he said as he handed us our rags and solvent. "And don't forget to put on your goggles – you don't want to get this stuff in your eyes."

I put on the mechanic coveralls that were two sizes too big, fire goggles and gloves. Our job was to degrease the undercarriage of the fire trucks. It was well over 100 degrees outside and even hotter under the truck with its underbelly just inches from my face. The underside of the truck was a complete mystery with mazes of metal, hoses, and other mechanical parts that were encased with a half an inch of black grease. With my rags, solvent and a chisel, I worked scraping and wiping away the thick, black, sticky goo. It was stifling hot and the smell of solvent was nauseating. The grease and solvent dripped down on my sweaty face and burned like hell. Every 15 minutes I crawled out from under the truck to get a breath of fresh air. Gomez and I worked together with him on one end of the truck and me on the other. Out of boredom we got into grease flinging fights as if we didn't have enough grease dripping in our faces. After a day of disgusting degreasing, I wished I was back to sweeping pine needles.

A fire station wasn't complete without the fire trucks and since they were our main tool for fighting fires, we took pride in keeping them clean and in working order. Fire trucks were always getting bombarded with fire retardant and grime from smoke and dusty roads, so we kept them waxed which helped with keeping the paint in prime condition. Up to this point, we still hadn't been called to a fire so they weren't in bad shape but we washed and waxed them anyway. I didn't mind because I would much rather have been working on top of the truck in the open air than underneath with the solvent and hot grime.

The station was on about 12 acres of land with lots of lawn that had to be mowed, and I volunteered to work the riding lawn mower every chance I got. I loved riding the mower since I was alone and nowhere near Compton or Singer. I got to sit on my butt for a few hours under the pine trees and it was wonderful. Our busy work was never-ending. We pulled nails out of boards in the equipment yard, mopped and re-mopped the barracks and dining building, scrubbed the kitchen, bathrooms and cleaned out the tool shed. When the radio crackled to life we stopped what we were doing and waited for our station to be called. It was always someone else, so we'd sigh and continued with our work.

The month of June seemed to last forever and our only dispatch was to cover for other nearby stations that were called out on fires. I was starting to think that we would never get called and my entire summer was going to be spent as a janitor/maintenance worker in a cool firefighter uniform.

SIX
Called Out

I learned to cook at Whitmore, something that would have amazed my mother. Growing up, I would have rather walked barefoot on glass than hang out in the kitchen. I took a cooking class in high school and the only thing I remembered was how to fry an egg. At the fire station, we all took turns cooking for the entire crew. I was completely freaked out at the idea of cooking for a bunch of people, especially being the only girl. I hoped that they didn't expect me to whip up something like good-ole mom would make. These guys were in for a big surprise. On my first day of cooking duty, I reluctantly crawled out of bed an hour before everyone else to start breakfast. It was still dark as I stumbled around and found my way to the showers and then to the dinning hall to get going on the daunting task of feeding the masses.

Behind the dining area there was a commercial sized kitchen with super sized appliances and a pantry of food held in gargantuan-sized packages and cans. I looked around the pantry filled with food. Scratching my head, I tried to figure out what I was going to make. I grabbed one of the huge packages of pancake mix and read the directions. Just mix with water. This sounded easy enough, however measuring the portions for an army was a little confusing, so I just poured the powder into a large mixing bowl and added water. I pretty much "eyeballed" the thickness of the batter. Firing up the industrial-sized griddle, I proceeded to make pancakes the size of dinner plates. On another griddle, I cooked big thick slabs of bacon and my specialty, fried eggs. When I was done, the kitchen looked like a breakfast bomb exploded as there was pancake mix and bacon grease splattered everywhere.

I wasn't a coffee drinker and had never made coffee before. I poured massive amounts of ground coffee into the giant percolator, again "eyeballing" the amount of water to use and turned it on. The coffee poured out thick as tar and tasted just as bad. As I was setting the table to present my feast, the crew started to file into the dinning room. "Smells great," said Mathers. "Don't drink the coffee," I warned. They all wolfed down my giant doughy undercooked pancakes. Wow! This crowd was easy to please! As we ate like hungry bears in silence, the fire radio suddenly came to life. First, a series of tones came through with a sing song melody followed by the dispatcher calling out trucks from crews closer to Redding. About five minutes later, another round of stations and trucks were called to this same fire. We continued to chow down on my monster pancake breakfast and chattered that something big was happening in Redding. We figured it was too far away for Whitmore to get called. The Plectron went off again, and surprisingly it was the Whitmore tone followed by my truck number, 2475. We took one last hurried bite of our pancakes and beat feet to the truck and scrambled into our gear. This was really happening – our first real fire!

As Abbott took the driver's seat with Mathers riding shotgun, I jumped in the back with Stackmore and Gomez. As the truck lumbered its way onto the highway, we frantically finished putting on our Nomex suits, helmets and other gear.

Finally settling into our seats and buckled in, we all sat in silence staring wide eyed through our plastic woodshop goggles as we flew down the road with the siren blaring. We traveled like this for almost an hour into Redding where a major brush and grass fire was burning out of control. During the ride, I had plenty of time to go over what I had learned in my brief grass fire training, which wasn't much. Many different scenarios and "what-ifs" rushed through my head during the ride. Just like my first call to the truck accident, I was very nervous about what I would to find when I got to this fire. Was it going to be scary? Will I be able to handle the job at hand? Did I remember everything I learned, anything at all? I looked down at my gloved hands and they seemed so small. By God they were *small*. I glanced over at Stackmore and Gomez who were staring straight ahead expressionless. Were they scared too? I couldn't tell.

As we got closer to Redding, we could clearly see the big plume of smoke just a few miles west of town. By the size of the smoke, we could tell the fire was quite large and spreading. We finally arrived on the scene and there were many fire trucks lined up with crew members scurrying about yanking hose here and there. Trees and brush burned in big balls of flame and airplanes flew overhead dropping fire retardant. I had heard of these planes in my fire classes, but I never imagined them to be so massive.

The Grumman S-2A air tanker, with a wingspan of 70 feet and huge engines and propellers on each of these wings, was an ex-Navy plane that was used in submarine warfare before they were purchased by CDF for firefighting purposes. Outfitted with tanks that carried 800 gallons of fire retardant called Borate, the S-2A could fly fast and low and covered a large area with retardant. We were told to "hit the deck" meaning to lay flat on our stomachs with our arms covering our heads when we heard the Borate bombers coming. The red, thick, sticky Borate dropped out of the bomb bay doors with great force that would knock you down if you weren't prepared.

Once we found our place on the fire line, we jumped out of the truck and turned on the water pump. This fire was much bigger than our small training grass fire as the flames whipped high over our heads as large bushes burned all around us. Abbott yelled out orders and it was hard to hear him over the overpowering sound of the fire, planes and the roaring pumps from all of the engines on the scene. As we quickly grabbed hose and hand tools, Stackmore just stood there with a dumb look on his face. Abbott screamed at him. "Get on that line Stackmore." After a month of hounding Stackmore to just do "busy work" correctly, easygoing Abbott's patience had run thin with this kid. Stackmore went over to the truck and started fumbling around the hose bin. It took way too long and Abbott pushed Stackmore aside and started to drag hose from the truck while Gomez grabbed onto the nozzle. I jumped behind Gomez and together we pulled out the big hose and marched toward the roaring inferno.

Stackmore was nowhere to be found and I just assumed he was wandering around with his thumb up his ass. The heat and smoke from the training fire was intense, but this was much worse. As we got closer, Gomez opened up the nozzle and a great force of water spewed out towards the burning bushes. The water seemed to make the flames angrier and bigger. We just kept the water on one spot until the flames died down then hit another spot of roaring flames. This fire was hot and downright painful as we had to stand at one hot spot for a long time before the water would eventually work.

Gomez and I chased each hot spot until we ran out of hose, then Abbott would move the truck closer to the fire so we could keep walking forward, slowly knocking out flames. As we worked intently on the task at hand, I heard a rumbling heading our way. Suddenly, I saw Gomez throw himself onto the dirt. What was he doing? I briefly looked up and got a glimpse of the underbelly of what looked like a huge whale. The plane was so low; I could see every detail down to the rivets that held it together. I stood there staring in awe when my brain kicked in and said "hit the deck dummy." I landed in the dirt with a thud on top of the hose and the big plane flew right over us releasing the load of sticky red slime out of the bomb bay doors.

It felt as if someone was hitting me repeatedly with a stick and I felt a sharp stinging sensation through my clothes as the heavy fire retardant hit us with extreme force. Gomez and I lay on the ground for a few seconds until we were sure the fire retardant had completely finished falling from the sky. This seemed to take awhile since the goo kept falling after the plane was long gone. I looked over at Gomez who was half-red and half-yellow and he had a "what the hell" look on his face. We immediately pointed to each other and burst out laughing. Looking around I realized that everything and everyone around us was soaked in red goo, including our fire truck. I knew we'd be busy washing and waxing it when we got back to the station. After a few of these bombing runs, the fire was quickly controlled and our job was to take the hose and put out the little flare-ups that sprouted here and there. Putting out a raging fire was dangerous, sometimes chaotic, but it was also exciting. What wasn't fun was the mop-up. The mop-up consisted of making sure that nothing was left smoldering after the main firefighting job was accomplished.

Mop-up was hot, nasty, smelly, tedious and very boring. When I was actually fighting the fire, everything happened so fast; I just dealt with the heat and pain. During mop-up up the adrenaline was no longer pumping and I thought I would die in my layers of clothing and Nomex. This part of the job went painfully slow as I raked the ashes and turned over logs while Gomez squirted each smoldering pile with water. If a log was smoking, we took an axe to it and made sure nothing was burning in the middle. I turned over the ash; Gomez soaked it, and so on, and so on and so on.

I looked around at the huge burn that spread over 150 acres. "This is going to take us forever to mop up," I sighed under my breath as I continued rake. The sun started to set and a few lucky crews were released to go back to their stations. Gomez and I raked and wet down ash well into the night. Apparently, the rule was that crews such as ours who were "late to the party" were the last to leave. I was starving and I thought about those doughy pancakes that had long been digested. I also had to pee. I looked around the burned landscape and any form of bushes that would have been my refuge were now sticks coming out of the ground not offering any form of privacy. Even if there was a secluded place for me to pee, I would have had to strip down two layers of clothing. This little scenario never once played out in my mind back in that fire class. I wasn't about to ask and be "that pain in the ass girl," so I held it for three more hours. When we finally got released, my bladder screamed all the way from Redding to Whitmore and every bump was excruciating. It was 10:00 p.m. when we made it back to the station and I sprinted to the barracks to make my bladder happy. I joined the rest of the crew in the dining hall and with our fire gear still on, Mathers and I cleared up the breakfast mess and whipped out some bread and lunch meat.

Stackmore, still pouting from the tongue lashing by Abbott disappeared into the barracks as soon as the trucks were parked. I wondered why that goofball hadn't quit by now. He wasn't cutting it and was driving the bosses crazy. There was an upside to having Stackmore around though; all of the attention was taken off me and put onto him! It appears that his blundering was even more annoying than having a girl around! At least no one had to tell me twice to do something and I worked like hell trying to prove myself.

The fire trucks lined up and ready to go!
Circa 1978

SEVEN

Four Boys, a Girl and a Weirdo Station Life

I was convinced there was something fundamentally wrong with Stackmore. He didn't seem to understand simple directions and I thought he was completely lazy. His work was half-ass and the bosses were always dogging him to get back to work. When it was his turn to sweep pine needles, I caught him leaning on his broom staring out into space for several minutes at a time. As soon as he noticed he was being watched he quickly went back to sweeping. I thought he was taking naps under the truck when it was his turn to degrease. He was really getting on all of our nerves and I prayed I didn't have to depend on his sorry-ass.

This was one of the hottest summers on record with the heat reaching up to 116 degrees. At almost 3000 feet, Whitmore wasn't far enough up in elevation to escape the high temperatures and it had been well over 100 degrees for over ten days. With the heat came sweat, and an ice-cold shower at the end of the day was a treat. Stackmore, however, wasn't showering consistently. I didn't think that he fully understood personal hygiene. He started to get pretty ripe and the guys gave him a hard time about showering.

"Stackmore, if you don't get that stink off you, we are going to hit you with the hose," said Captain Harris after breakfast one day.

"Yeah, the big one, and it ain't gonna feel very good," said Compton and for once I sided with him. Stackmore stunk and this was just the beginning of his craziness. It never cooled down at night and the barracks swamp cooler worked overtime. Stackmore's bed was across the room from mine and directly across from Mathers. I finally started to doze off when the scratching began. Scratch, scratch, scratch. Stackmore incessantly scratched like a dog with fleas. I didn't know what body part he was scratching but it was nonstop.

"Stackmore!" yelled Mathers. "Will you please take care of that shit?" I put the pillow over my head to drown out the scratching.

Mathers threw one of his boots across the room. "Will you fucking stop it?" He got out of bed to retrieve his boot and stood over Stackmore.

"I can't help it. I've got jock itch and I don't have anything to put on it," whined Stackmore.

"Well if you would fucking bathe once in a while" yelled Compton.

"What the hell is all the yelling?" Singer stood in the door way and turned on the lights. I flung the covers over my head, not wanting any part of this weird guy stuff. Jock itch? Was it catching? Could I get it? I didn't want to know and hid like a scared rabbit suffocating under my blanket.

"Stackmore, I'll go into town and get you something for it in the morning, but you better start taking a shower," yelled Singer.

"My feet are pretty messed up too, can you get me something for that?

Singer groaned, flicked off the light and stomped out of the room.
As soon as Singer left, boots and anything not nailed down flew from every bed like rockets towards Stackmore.

"Come on you guys, I can't help it, it really itches." plead Stackmore.
I made a mental note to ask Mathers about this business of jock itch and what the hell it was.

Everyday at 5.00 p.m. we were officially excused from our busy work, and after dinner, we got to do anything we wanted, without leaving the station of course, until its lights out at 10.00 p.m. A basketball hoop was at the far end of the parking lot and the guys were always playing H.O.R.S.E which was a one-on-one type of game of free throws. Each person took a turn making a shot at the basket and if you missed you got a letter. The first to get all the letters to spell H.O.R.S.E, lost. They asked me if I wanted to play a couple of times, but I felt too intimidated and politely declined.

One night Mathers was out by himself shooting baskets. "You want to try," he asked. Since it was just Mathers, I decided to try my hand at shooting some hoops. I took the ball and completely surprised myself by making a basket my very first try. While playing, we changed the name of our game to P.R.I.C.K.; I guess we thought it would be hilarious that the loser would be called Prick. Since I sucked at basketball, it was no surprise that I got the losing title of Prick immediately. Eventually Mathers morphed the title to "Little Prick" just for me and it stuck. Now, most girls would have been offended to be called Little Prick. Not me! I was proud of the fact that I "won" this title fair and square by losing at basketball. Of course, Compton quickly got on the band wagon of calling me Little Prick and coming from him, it grated on my nerves a little! After working at the station and enduring Singer and Compton, I kind of became a "Little Prick" in my demeanor so the name was fitting.

After enduring ribbing and snide comments as well as performing endless grimy work and dealing with snoring, scratching guys through the night, I was changing and eventually became a hardened little prick. I started to really take on the roll as "one of the boys." As much as I was reminded by one of my co-workers every day that I was a girl that had no business being at Whitmore, I went out of my way NOT to look like a girl. I wore my collection of big farmer-type ball hats that said John Deere, CAT or some other manly slogan. I also carried a big switchblade knife on my belt, not so much for protection but just to look tough. I did these things to deflect any attention off me and tried my best to blend in with the crowd of men. I figured that if I did eventually have to work among thousands of men and male prisoners on a big fire, I had already perfected my part as the little butch girl. I wanted my persona to say don't mess with Little Prick! Mathers and I played many games of P.R.I.C.K. during the evenings in which I lost every time. When we passed each other at the station I yelled, "Hey Prick!" He yelled back "Hey Little Prick." I finally felt like I was actually fitting in – somewhat.

Some nights I would play long games of rummy and poker with Gomez and Brooks in the dinning hall. Brooks was quiet and smart and was very interesting to talk to once you got him going. He was a problem solver and I wished he was on my truck, but instead, I was stuck with the likes of Stackmore.

Singer gave Stackmore his much needed medicine for his itching issues, but he still wasn't showering. I made doubly sure I wore my rubber thongs when I took a shower, and I used extra bleach when I had to scrub the bathroom floors. I made sure to kill all of

Stackmore's nasty germs. With his medicine working, he slept like a baby. Only now, we had to deal with his constant snoring. The other guys snored, but oh my God this guy sounded like a chainsaw.

"Shut the fuck up Stackmore." A boot went flying across the room.

"Whaaaaaat?" whined Stackmore.

"Stackmore, turn over on your side," I said. I brought my pillow around my head and ears. This guy had to go. How the hell were we to get any sleep the rest of the summer with this freak in the barracks?

Finally, Stackmore left the station for his two days off and we got a couple of nights of uninterrupted sleep. We hoped and prayed that he didn't come back and you could hear a collective groan when his car pulled into the station. There was no getting rid of stinky Stackmore. His hygiene was so nasty that we refused to let him cook and we'd flip a coin to see who would take Stackmore's kitchen duty. At least Singer made sure that Stackmore had to do some back breaking work in lieu of cooking.

"Cornett, you and Stackmore do some tool sharpening today," said Singer. To my disgust, I got to sit with stinky Stackmore at the tool shed. This was the first time that I had any one-on-one time with Stackmore, as I purposely stayed away from him. A little part of me did feel sorry for Stackmore because he was well out of his element as a firefighter. On the other hand, my pity would go out the window when he didn't take initiative to do anything. He proved himself completely worthless on our first real fire which scared me. Having some one-on-one time with Stackmore, I told him he really needed to shape up and that I believed the crew was really close to dragging him off into the woods and beating the living shit out of him. Stackmore just rolled his eyes, shrugged his shoulders and kept on filing his shovel, doing a crappy job by the way.

I counted down the minutes on Sunday night when at 5:00 p.m. I could get in my car, crank up my stereo and hightail it out of that madhouse for two whole days. I was literally homeless on my days off, so I had to get creative in my accommodations. I kept my backpacking gear in my car and I was well equipped to live outdoors if I had to. I secured a regular camping spot in the mountains above the station that was next to a creek; however, I really never felt that it was far enough off the beaten path. I never knew what crazy human would happen upon my tent and find a lone girl sleeping there. Trying to find a more secluded spot, I drove my car up a very remote logging road that soon turned into a rugged trail. Realizing I couldn't go any further, I tried to turn my car around and managed to get it high-centered over a big dirt mound. With my back wheels not touching the ground, I abandoned my car and hiked out in search of someone who could help me. It was starting to get dark and after hiking for about three miles, I found a house tucked back into the woods. I prayed that this wasn't where the serial camper killer lived! The man who answered the door was surprised to see a girl in a CDF uniform standing on his front porch. After explaining my predicament, he was nice enough to give me a ride back to my car and helped pull it off the mound of dirt. With no place to go for the night, I went back to my familiar camp spot. I needed to find more permanent accommodations for the rest of the summer.

EIGHT
The Lonely Lookout

T rying to find friends to stay with in Redding was difficult since most of them had moved home with their parents for the summer. On my next days off and with camping no longer an option, I decided to make the trip up to Southfork Mountain Lookout to finally see the face behind the voice with the southern drawl on the fire radio. I thought that I might be able to talk her into letting me camp there for the weekend. Southfork Mountain is the second highest peak on the western side of Redding, on the opposite side of the valley from Whitmore.

There were several hundred lookout towers in California that were manned during fire season. The fire lookout had a very lonely job since they lived in this tower on top of a mountain completely isolated from civilization five days a week, 24 hours a day. The two-way radio was the only communication the lookout had with the outside world. When the sun went down, the lookout was officially off the clock, but they had to stay at their post so at the break of dawn, they were ready with their binoculars to search for smoke. Once they saw smoke, they used a device called an Osborne Fire Finder to figure out its approximate location. The fire finder was a big, flat circular table that sat in the middle of the lookout's small living space.

On the face of the table was a topography map of the surrounding area within sight of the tower which was approximately 40 miles or so. The fire finder had a rim that was graduated in degrees with a set of crosshairs at the edge of the table that the lookout could freely move around 360 degrees. When the lookout spotted smoke, he/she looked through the crosshairs of the fire finder and moved the wheel around to mark the spot of the smoke using the map and the azimuth.[1] The lookout then called in the approximate coordinates of the smoke to the fire dispatch center in Redding who in turn dispatched the appropriate fire station.

With Jackson Browne's "Running on Empty" playing on my new in-dash cassette player that piped through my also newly installed speakers, I drove my Plymouth Valiant up the steep dirt road that winded with switchbacks up Southfork Mountain. The views were spectacular.

The lookout had no idea that I was coming up to her tower. I made sure that I was in my CDF uniform so she wouldn't think I was some crazy stalker. I made it up to the top of the mountain to find an extremely tall metal tower with a little hut at the top. The tower building was like a fortress with big metal doors at the bottom which led to the stairs that went up to the hut. Antennas and lightning rods stuck out of the top of the tower with another huge antennae tower right next to the main lookout tower.

---

[1] The horizontal angular distance from a reference direction, usually the northern point of the horizon, to the point where a vertical circle through a celestial body intersects the horizon, usually measured clockwise. Sometimes the southern point is used as the reference direction, and the measurement is made clockwise through 360°.

As I got out of my car, I craned my neck and squinted my eyes in the blaring sun looking for signs of life way up in the hut.

"Hey down there," said a familiar voice that I had grown to know so well.

"Hi I'm Jan and I'm a firefighter over at Whitmore, can I come up?" "I'm Gloria, door's open, but watch out for rattlers, they love to hang out on the steps," she yelled from her catwalk.

Rattlesnakes??? My mind went wild with visions of huge slithering snakes ready to pounce on me when I opened the big metal door. Completely freaking out, I opened the door with extreme caution. It was dark and it took a few seconds for my eyes to somewhat adjust but it was still pretty dark. With each cautious heart-pounding step, I looked around for any signs of snakes. Finally making it to the top, thankfully, without a rattlesnake encounter, I was greeted by an older lady with short gray hair, a friendly smile and a very jovial personality. Gloria had worked in this lookout tower for 25 years and everyone in the fire service knew her and her stories. She was legendary.

A favorite story among firefighters was the tale on how Gloria got her nickname, Hawkeye.[1] It wasn't because she was good at what she did and had spotted many fires over the years; it was because of one incident where she accidentally called in a fire that was completely impossible for her to see from Southfork Mountain.

One day, Gloria spotted a fire way off in the distance. Using the fire finder she called the coordinates into dispatch and told them that she had spotted smoke. She went outside on the catwalk with her binoculars and didn't see it anymore; it was gone! She went back into the tower and saw the smoke again and double checked its

---

[1] Thank you Chris W. for reminding me of this story!

location with the fire finder. In the mean time, crews were dispatched exactly where she said there was a fire, and upon their arrival, they found a resident illegally burning a very small controlled fire. The fire was so small, they couldn't figure out how the heck it was spotted by Southfork lookout that was miles away. It was impossible. As it turned out, Gloria didn't see the fire at all, there was no way she could have, even with binoculars. What she saw was a smudge on the glass of her tower window and the fire she called out was mere coincidence. From that day on, everyone called her Hawkeye.

"Welcome to my little piece of heaven," she said shaking my hand vigorously. "Did you see any snakes? They like to curl up in the corners." I didn't think heaven had snakes and I cringed at the thought of having to go back down those stairs. Suddenly I forgot all about the snakes when I got my first glimpse of the unbelievable 360-degree view out of the very large windows that wrapped the living quarters of the tower. I swore I could hear an angel choir singing as my eyes feasted on the unbelievable view. Gloria was right, this was heaven. To the west, I could see Whiskey Town Lake in its entirety, the grand peaks of the Trinity Alps and the Pacific Coastal range of mountains beyond that. Looking to the north, I was stunned by the view and enormity of Mount Shasta and Shasta Lake below. The eastern view stretched across the tip of the Sacramento Valley with Mt. Lassen standing guard. The southern view stretched down the Sacramento Valley.

"What station did you say you were from?" asked Gloria.

"Whitmore," I replied still gawking out of the windows. "I was wondering if I could spend the weekend up here and learn about being a lookout."

"Sure thing, if you don't mind sleeping on the catwalk."

"Not at all, I have my sleeping bag and I brought my own food."
The little living quarters was simple with a single bed, stove, sink, small table and the centerpiece and most important item in the tower, the Osborne Fire Finder. It was 7:00 p.m. when I reached the tower, and the sun was blaring its 100 degree heat.

Gloria was still on the clock and continuously scanned the valley with her binoculars as she asked me all sorts of questions about my life at Whitmore. My lessons as a lookout started immediately and she taught me how to use the fire finder and gave me brief instruction on the use of the radio. Gloria showed me the landmarks and taught me how she figured approximate distances. "See that hill over there, that's about 20 miles from downtown Redding," she said, never taking her binoculars away from her eyes. "Once you learn all of the landmarks, it's easy to figure out where the smokes are and makes using the fire finder a lot easier," she continued. We did this for the next two hours until it was completely dark and the only thing we could see was the glimmering lights from Redding below. At sunset, Gloria got on the radio and signed off for the night. I headed down to my car to get my gear making sure I shined my flashlight on each step looking for those dreaded rattlesnakes.

A person could get stir crazy with no human contact for days on end, and Gloria was starving for conversation. Now that she was officially off the clock, she proceeded to talk my ear completely off my head. It was like a switch was flipped. She talked non-stop.

I heard all about her life, where she grew up, her husband, her kids, her gazillion fire stories, how she shot rattlesnakes off of the steps with her .22 rifle for fun, the biggest rattlesnake she ever saw, the time she was almost bit by a rattlesnake, the mountain lions she shot at, the hippies that found their way to the tower that she had to run off, the fire that almost took out her tower, every pet that she ever owned, stories about her crazy family and on and on and on.

It was almost 11 p.m. when Gloria finally said, "Well, better hit the hay, the sun comes up really early." Gloria made her way back inside the hut and I was left alone on the catwalk in the cool night air to take in the blinking lights in the valley below as I finally fell asleep.

I woke up in a sweat as the sun was just coming over the horizon. It was already blazing hot and I was lying on the eastern side of the tower right in the direct sun on the metal catwalk. I heard the fire radio come to life as dispatch did the morning roll call of all the fire stations and lookout towers. Gloria was up and scurried about the hut cooking breakfast on her little stove and talking on the radio. As I made my way into the cool tower, she handed me a cup of coffee, a pair of binoculars, and we instantly got to work scoping out the valley. I soon realized that the days were extremely long in a lookout tower and I couldn't image how much longer the days would feel when you had absolutely no one to talk to.

Because of the long heat wave, the Redding basin was very smoggy and it was hard to decipher things. Through the brown haze I thought I spotted something in my binoculars. All excited I ran around the catwalk where Gloria was looking at the mountains to the west. "Well, let's have a look-see," she said. I pointed to the direction of where I last saw the smoke as Gloria scanned the land with her high powered binoculars. "Don't see nuthin'," she said. "Sometimes you get a poof of black smoke from a diesel truck. If it's gone in a few seconds, you got nuthin but exhaust. Your eyes can really play tricks on you and lots of things can look like smoke. You really have to keep your eyes on it for a minute and time it. If it's consistent, you got smoke." This took some getting used to as many things looked like smoke from miles away.

I was afraid if Gloria hadn't taken a second look at my "smokes," I would have been sending fire crews all over the valley on wild goose chases.

Around 5 p.m. the weekend replacement lookout Ann came to relieve Gloria. With a flash, Gloria said her quick goodbyes, hurried down the steps to her waiting husband and the only thing left was a trail of dust down the dirt road.

Ann, who was a little older than I, had worked at the lookout for five years. She had been a full-time lookout for the first two years, but didn't like being stuck on the mountain by herself for five days straight. She told me she liked being a weekend warrior. My night with Ann was much more enjoyable as she wasn't so manic and didn't feel the need to talk me to death. We sat on the catwalk, talked about women in the Forestry, and went to bed much earlier than the night before. I spent another day learning the ropes of being a lookout from Ann. "OK, I got something," Ann said as she ran into the hut to dial in the smoke on the fire finder. As she positioned the wheel towards the east, I looked through my binoculars to try to find what she was seeing. I saw a thin column of gray smoke trailing high into the haze on the other side of the valley. Just as Ann reached for the radio to call it in, the lookout on the north side of the valley beat her to it and gave dispatch the coordinates from his vantage point. There seemed to be a little competition among the lookouts and there was a race to be the first to call in smoke sightings to dispatch. Ann looked a little miffed as she waited for the other lookout to complete the call so that she could call in the coordinates from her vantage point.

As the lookouts competed for the "first call" it actually did help the fire crews to have more than one tower spy the same smoke so they could get the most accurate location using two fire finders since the coordinates could be narrowed down. With the smoke called in, fire crews were sent to a small grass fire that burned a couple of acres which was quickly extinguished.

As the day drew to an end with the sun dipping over the horizon, my "shift" as a lookout ended and I had to get back to my station. Holding my breath, I slowly climbed down the dark stairs of the tower once again intensely looking for rattlesnakes in which I was convinced were ready to strike. Whew, no snakes! I opened the big double metal doors and once again on solid ground started my drive down the windy lookout mountain road to the valley below.

Back at the station, it was life as usual with the constant busywork. As the long summer days went on and on, we tried to make the best of our situation by playing practical jokes on each other, especially on Stackmore, staying off Singer's radar and doing our sweeping, mowing, etc, etc, etc. The massive heat wave in Northern California marched on and the 110 degree weather showed no signs of letting up. The crew was really getting grouchy and we were about at our breaking point with boredom. Something interesting had to happen soon or we would have eventually killed each other.

NINE

The Fire Tour

After of a month of no excitement, I wished I was working at a kid's camp and not scraping grease from the belly of a fire engine in 100 degree weather. Did I make a mistake about this firefighting thing? I mean come on! Where were all the damned fires? Singer was acting more like a prison guard than a boss and we all did the happy dance whenever he left for his days off. Captain Harris was a really nice guy, but he spent most of his time in the office and we rarely saw him during the day. He dropped by the barracks once in a while and shot the shit with us, but it was Singer who was our day-to-day boss and slave master most days.

It was the second week of July when I was awakened by a bright light. Singer was at the doorway of our barracks hollering for us to get geared up, we had a call. I bolted out of bed, wondering why none of us heard the Plectron and scrambled for my clothes. By now, I had gotten really good at changing clothes under the clothes that I had on as to not flash skin to the boys. I quickly got ready and ran out to the truck in complete darkness. Singer had already pulled our truck into the yard, and the entire forest looked like blinking Christmas trees from the red rotating and flashing light dome on top of the truck.

We headed off into the night to look for a fire that was reported just a few miles from the station. We drove up and down the road hitting the forest and the surrounding meadows with a spotlight and never did find the reported fire. The only thing we saw were deer meandering around in the cover of darkness. The deer froze like statues not sure what to make of the spotlight upon them.

We spent some time traversing up and down the road harassing the grazing deer with our light and still found nothing. Mathers got on the radio and announced to dispatch that the fire was UTL (unable to locate) finally, we headed back to the station and warm bunks to finish off our night's slumber. Before we reached the station, another call came in from dispatch telling us we were to cover a station in the Lassen Forest area which was 100 miles away. There was a huge fire burning in the Modoc National Forest and outside crews were needed to cover the stations that were almost abandoned by their crews who were off fighting those fires.

Off we went into the night with Singer driving, Mathers riding shotgun, Stackmore, Gomez and myself on the back, out in the open, for the next 100 miles. It was a hot night and for a while it felt good to ride in the open air. Lassen Forest was about two hours away and we climbed over some pretty big mountain passes to get there. As we drove higher in elevation it started to get really cold. We were only wearing our short sleeve cotton shirts, green pants and our Nomex suits, which weren't all that thick. We had on our gloves, helmets and goggles, but all of this gear wasn't enough to keep the cold air from chilling our bones.

The temperature had dropped to about 40 degrees and traveling down the road at 55 miles per hour, the wind chill made it about ten degrees lower. My teeth chattered as I hunched over with my head between my knees to keep out of the freezing wind. Stackmore drove us crazy with his whining and screaming that he was cold. Gomez punched Stackmore in the arm to get him to shut the hell up. All of my muscles were tense and I tried to get my mind off of the cold and pain by singing 99 bottles of beer on the wall at the top of my lungs. My singing got Stackmore to shut up and he looked at me as if I had lost my mind. Gomez laughed and sang along. "Sing Stackmore," I yelled. "Yeah fucking sing," yelled Gomez punching Stackmore in the arm again. We got through all 99 bottles of beer and started the song over again and then moved on to other songs to keep our minds off of freezing to death.

Stackmore still whimpered like a baby and Gomez socked him in the arm for the tenth time. For the next hour and half we rode shivering until the sun came up providing some warmth. Finally arriving at our destination, we tried to climb down off of the truck but it was hard to move our frozen legs.

"Come on you big baby, you can get down now," Gomez said to Stackmore completely disgusted.

"Get a little cold back there Little Prick?" said Mathers smiling.

"Asshole," I replied as I stumbled about trying to get the feeling back into my legs. It felt good to be basking in the sunlight as my body slowly thawed.

The fire station, which would be our home for a few days, was big and deserted with only a couple of crew members remaining. The rest of the crew and trucks were off fighting the big Modoc fire and it was unknown when they would be back. As we walked into the spacious dining room, I saw a girl with long hair wearing jeans and a tee-shirt working in the kitchen. This girl wasn't wearing a CDF uniform and I wondered if she'd been hired to be the station cook. Dang, these guys were lucky! I soon learned that her name was Crystal and she was a lookout at one of the towers. There were two girls that worked at nearby towers and on their days off, they had a place to stay at the CDF station if they wanted.

I went to a lookout tower because I had nowhere to go on my days off and these gals went to the CDF station to spend their weekends. Go figure! The lookout girls, Crystal and Mary were college students who lived in the San Francisco Bay Area a few hundred miles away and going home on the weekends was difficult. For years, the CDF station had accommodated the lookout tower workers with a place to stay. As soon as Crystal saw me, she skipped out of the kitchen and without a word and with a huge smile grabbed me by the arm and whisked me away from the guys. "Oh man, am I glad to see you!" she said as we meandered through the station halls.

She took me to a large room in the back that had two bunk beds. "This is our room; you can have the top bunk." I had died and gone to heaven. I finally got to have a night of sleep where I didn't have to listen to Stackmore scratch and snore. Crystal was excited to see me as well since her days were spent either alone, or with all of the guys at the station.

I told her I that I didn't have a toothbrush or a change of clothes since we left Whitmore in the middle of the night. I was so dog tired from freezing my ass off in the back of that truck with no sleep - I couldn't wait to get out of my gear. She lent me an oversized t-shirt and a pair of sweats and I hopped into a much needed shower. Crystal jumped in her truck, and 20 minutes later showed back up with a little goodie bag filled with toothpaste, toothbrush, comb, brush, candy and some hair clips since my hair was growing out and I was complaining that my bangs were in my eyes. For a few hours I got to feel like a girl again while I brushed out my hair and had mindless girl talk with Crystal.

Since we were "visiting" this station, Singer didn't make us do busy work. Thank God! Crystal and I spent time in our own little "girls' oasis" sharing our war stories of the summer. She told me all about being a lookout and I told her my story of being the first and only girl at Whitmore. I shared with her all the details about Compton, Singer and the crazy Stackmore which made her double over in laughter.

We ended up staying at the Lassen station for four days and I was grateful that I had the lookout girls taking care of me. Since I was on duty the entire time and not allowed to leave the station, Mary and Crystal would go to the store and bring back magazines, candy and all sorts of goodies. The atmosphere of this station was much like a college dorm and the engineer on duty was very laid back, the complete opposite of Singer. I had no comparisons of fire stations and I figured that all CDF stations operated like Whitmore and had a "Singer" in their midst. This wasn't the case at Lassen, they had a great time.

The Twin Fire in the Modoc Forest grew to 23,000 acres and our little crew was called to man another station about an hour up the highway. Crystal and I exchanged hugs and addresses and she gave me a sack containing all of the goodies that she was able to get for me during my stay. I was sad to be leaving this wonderful happy station. Singer was even tolerable this past week and I wondered if the laid back environment of the Lassen crew rubbed off on him....nah.

We continue to travel from station to station, being called to fires along the way. We only got to stay at these stations just long enough to get gas, something to eat and use the bathroom then we were back on the road again. I was getting good at sleeping sitting up in the back of the truck and thank God we traveled during the daylight while it was warm. We hadn't showered since we left the Lassen station and we were pretty ripe. Sprinkle smoke and soot along with days of sweat and you had a pretty smelly group of people.

After about two weeks of touring several CDF stations, we made one final stop in the small town of Alturas. I was actually enjoying our little road trip and was glad that we didn't have to go back to Whitmore any time soon. The longer we stayed out on the road, the longer I got to avoid the day-in and day-out boredom and busy work that was waiting at Whitmore.

Alturas was in the far North/East corner of the state of California and there wasn't much around for miles. We were told that we would hold up there for a day or so, get showered and at least have one night of sleep in a bed. Again, we were spared with having to do any sort of busy work and we just sat around and waited for a fire call. As fun as the tour had been, we knew it was about to come to an end since the Twin Fire in the Modoc Forest was winding down and crews were returning to their regular stations. Just as we were loading up for our departure, we got a call to a grass fire on a ranch just outside of town. We rolled up to a big cattle ranch to find a big pile of hay blazing with flames shooting high in the air. Once we got the fire out, Gomez and I did our usual routine of mop-up, raking and watering the smelly hay. A newspaper reporter from the local Alturas newspaper took our picture as Gomez raked and I watered down the sour smelling hay. I later got a copy of this photo when we got back to Whitmore and was miffed that the caption incorrectly said that the Alturas Volunteer Fire Department put out a hay fire on the Acre Ranch. The photo clearly shows Gomez raking with me holding the hose standing next to our truck 2475.

Towards the end of July, when the big fires in Modoc County were finally under control, we were sent back to Whitmore. The long ride home was actually quite nice since we traveled during the day and Stackmore was slept like a baby, relieving us from his usual constant sniveling and whining. I swear to God, I wanted to dump his ass off on the side of the road someplace. It was Sunday night when we rolled into the Whitmore and officially my day off. I quickly took a much needed shower and with fresh smelling civilian clothes I sprinted to my car. "So long suckers, I'm heading to Redding," I yelled as I peeled out of the parking lot.

I couldn't wait to get down to Redding and enjoy my much deserved days off in the land of civilization. However, this time I didn't go to the lookout tower to listen to Gloria's endless jabber and sleep on the catwalk, no sir! This time I was heading to a little town outside of Redding called Summit City to meet up with a fireman.

Mopping up a hay fire in Alturas
I'm on the right working the hose

Alturas Rural Volunteer firefighters take on the smoke to douse smouldering hay on the road between Akers Ranch and County Road 60 Monday after hay fell on the exhaust of a truck, torching both the hay and the truck.

Erroneous caption in the Alturas newspaper

TEN
Whitmore Fire
The Big One

S ummit City was a very small spec in the road North of Redding on the way to Shasta Dam. It consisted of a school, tackle and bait shop, a drive-in type of diner, a smattering of homes and a very small fire department with two full time paid firemen. The rest of the fire department was made up of volunteers. Chris, the captain of the Summit City Fire Department had no idea that I was about to show up at his fire house. I had met Chris in my firefighting class at Shasta College and ran into him later on a fire. Luckily for me he was extremely hospitable and we had a fabulous weekend together four wheeling in his Toyota Land Cruiser that we took all over the surrounding mountains. Chris grew up in San Francisco, but for a city kid, he was an outdoors kind of guy which was mandatory if you were to be my boyfriend. I didn't like the fancy types.

On day two of our first date weekend, we took a drive on the west side of the valley very near Southfork Lookout. Chris had his fire radio with him and in case he got a call, we could beat feet back to Summit City. As we 4-wheeled up the side of a mountain, we noticed a large column of smoke billowing from the mountains directly across the valley.

Chris's radio came to life as Southfork lookout called in the smoke which was starting to get larger by the second. Gloria had pinpointed the fire near the town of Whitmore. It figured that Whitmore would finally get a big call on my day off! We stood gazing across the valley at this huge plume of smoke that was rose several thousand feet into the air above the mountain range. Familiar tones sounded the hand held radio as Whitmore trucks were dispatched with my truck 2475 being one of them.

I felt helpless that I was so far away from my station. "I have to go." We jumped into the Land Cruiser and headed to Summit City. I quickly packed my car and drove back to Whitmore several hours before my weekend was to officially come to an end. I wasn't going to miss this call if I could help it. I drove my car like a maniac and was worried about getting pulled over for speeding.

"OK Ma'am, where's the fire?" my imaginary cop asked.

"But officer, there really is a fire, and I'm a firefighter and I really need to get to this fire."

"OK, sure...out of the car, you're under arrest."

I kept looking in my rear view mirror, imagining this conversation with the cop that was sure to pull me over. I made it back to Whitmore in record time only to find my truck long gone. Hey you missed your ride," quips Captain Harris. Dang it! I had been having a great time up in Summit City and I rushed back for nothing.

Disappointed, I stomped back over to the barracks and started to unload my stuff when I was told by a fire boss that I had to take out all of my belongings and put them in my car. We were officially kicked out of the barracks.

A huge fire camp was forming at Whitmore with trucks loaded with supplies, bulldozers, trailers, and a boat load of fire trucks and firefighters. "Pull your car around to the back yard and make sure it's locked up, we need to clear this area. Whitmore is now a command center and the barracks are for top brass," he said.

I wondered where in the heck I was supposed to sleep that night as big rig trucks pulled into the station and workers got busy setting up long tables around the camp. Truck after truck of fire crews arrived from all over the place. The rigs that really got my attention were the bus type trucks containing the grizzliest characters I had ever seen. I soon learned that these were the prisoner fire crews that I had heard about. There were hundreds of them. As our sleepy little station became a huge city, it started to hit me that I was one girl out of hundreds of men. I did my best to blend in the crowd but being so small, that wasn't an easy task.

Not long after I got my gear out of the barracks, I saw my truck 2475 come back into the station. I asked Mathers a ton of questions about the fire . Mathers told me the fire was only five miles down the road and cooking pretty good. He said it was started by a lightning strike that happened the day before during a storm that rolled through and it smoldered for a while before it really got going. There were a bunch of lightning strikes that hit all over the north part of the state from this storm. "We'd still be out there if we didn't have pump troubles." he said. "Get your gear ready, cuz we officially on the night crew."

As I walked to my car to get my gear, I passed through the area where the food service people were setting up. If I were to just happen upon this madness and didn't know that there was a fire someplace, I would have thought this was a big BBQ party. A very large refrigeration truck was parked in front of our kitchen building and all sorts of meats, produce, fresh fruits and soft drinks among other delicacies were unloaded and placed on the long tables. I heard that the fire camps were well supplied, but I hadn't imagined them being like a resort with every food item you desired at your disposal. The smell of large delicious steaks cooking on the many grills hit the air, and I was getting really hungry. "Cornett, we're loading up. Get your gear and let's go," said Mathers as he headed over to the garage to our truck. I dutifully left the smorgasbord behind and climbed onto my truck, and with much excitement and anticipation, I headed to my biggest fire yet.

California had been in such a drought for so long that the earth was extremely dry. We traveled on fire roads that were cut by bulldozers which became deep with powder dust. Even with my goggles and bandana over my face, the dust still found its way into my nose and lungs. As we made our way in the deep dust, we could smell the smoke but had a hard time seeing anything because of the red dust clouds that billowed behind the truck. We traveled like this for about twenty minutes before we jerked to a sudden stop. The dust cloud enveloped the back of the truck and I could barely see Mathers as he got out of the cab and walked towards us. "Everybody out, we have a flat tire." You have got to be kidding me! I was never going to see any fire at this rate. I had the worst luck. The guys quickly got out a jack, rounded up the spare and changed our tire. Having never changed a tire in my entire life, I had no idea what to do so, I took pictures with my little 110 instant camera that I decided to throw in my gear bag at the last minute. With the tire changed, we once again hit the dusty road.

It wasn't too much longer before we saw big flames lighting up the night sky. It started to get extremely smokey and my eyes burned like crazy. I would typically soak my bandana with water to filter out smoke, but in this dust, my bandana would have turned into a big mud flap - impossible to breathe through. Up ahead the pine trees and underbrush roared with fire. Seeing a 100-foot pine tree engulfed in flames in the night sky made me feel insignificant and small in the midst of this inferno, and I was amazed at how fast a huge pine tree burned. In a matter of a few seconds, the entire tree exploded from the ground to the very top with the flames leaping even higher into the sky.

We hurriedly got to work, pulling hose and grabbing hand tools. The low lying brush burned around us while we put water on anything within reach. As Gomez and I worked, I caught a glimpse of Stackmore and Singer in a heated argument back by the truck. Singer was mad as hell and had his finger in Stackmore's face. A day didn't go by without Stackmore getting his butt chewed out and today was no different. It was just another day with Stackmore, but this time we were in the middle of a big fire and his ineptness was completely intolerable and scary.

What I couldn't understand was why Singer hadn't fired him. Maybe Singer thought he could fix Stackmore in some weird way, but I personally didn't think that was possible. Stackmore had serious issues. I was convinced that this guy was going to get killed and possibly get me killed in the process. We were in a very intense situation and I kept a watchful eye on Stackmore more than ever.

The fire was really moving fast and trees were crowning on the ridge to our right. A crowning fire was dangerous and intense. This meant that the tops of the trees, which remember were from 100-200 feet tall, burned at the very tops spreading the fire rapidly from tree top to tree top. The only way to combat this type of fire was from the air. Borate bombers didn't fly at night so we didn't get the air support that we surely could have used. California has a variety of very large pine trees that grow in the Sierra Nevada. With a seven-year drought, these trees were dry and lacking in moisture. Some of them were completely dead or dying from beetle infestations. The forest had become a literal stick of old, volatile dynamite. The best we could do at this point was to keep the ground fire from spreading.

It was almost midnight when we finally got a break for dinner and Singer dug out the infamous C-rations that I had yet to experience. When I first started with CDF, we were issued a little metal can opener called a P-38 that we were told to put in our pocket or hook onto something. It was very important that we had this opener on us at all times. I had mine hooked onto my knife case and never had an opportunity to use it until now. The P-38 was 1 ½ inches long, with a little sharp hook that folded out. This handy dandy little tool was developed in 1942 and was Army issued.

C-rations had been around even longer, and I was pretty sure that these particular C-rations that I was about to eat were from the Vietnam war era. C-rations were introduced to the troops during

World War II, and soldiers could easily carry these little cans with them in combat when food wasn't readily available.

A typical box of C-rations held a can of mystery meat, a can of very dry crackers that also included a chocolate covered cracker of some sort, cheese spread, a can of mixed fruit cocktail, and sometimes a candy bar. I tried out my little P-38 and opened up the can of meat. It looked like pressed Spam and smelled foul. I tossed the can and opened the crackers. OK, these were much better and with the cheese spread, not so bad. The fruit tasted good and of course I chowed down on the candy bar. It wasn't exactly the steak I wanted back at fire camp, but I was starving and this little meal held me until morning where I knew a gourmet breakfast was waiting at the station. As we ate our c-rations, a pack of green Forest Service fire trucks flew by leaving us standing in huge thick clouds of red dust. Thanks guys, just what I needed, more mud clots up my nose and dirt in my fruit cup!

We continued to work throughout the night spraying water on smoldering trees and bushes. Just before dawn, we rolled up our hose and headed back down the dusty road to civilization. Our station, now a full-blown fire camp/command center, had grown into a virtual city with hundreds of firefighters and fire trucks. I spied a group of prisoners that looked worn out from a hard night of digging fire line. I was a little self conscious being the only girl among the hordes of men, especially the mean looking prisoners. Were they murderers or rapists? Were they all horny from being in prison and go crazy at the sight of a girl? When I got off the truck I put on my "Little Prick" act and strutted across the station acting bad ass with a "don't mess with me" attitude.

Soot covered crews were standing in the breakfast line, and others were laying all over the lawn that I had recently mowed. It was hot and the tired crews moved around on the lawn chasing the shade where they could. Since I was kicked out of the barracks, I had to use the extremely bad smelling portable toilets. It was over 1000 degrees in that little smelly box, so I quickly did my business and got the hell out of there before I died of toxic poisoning and heat stroke.

As I wandered around the station in awe of all of the activity and people milling about, I saw something spectacular! Females! They were with the Forest Service crews and it looks liked they were working on one of those green fire trucks that left is in the dust. Extremely excited to commune with my own kind, I walked over to their truck to introduce myself. "Hey, welcome to Whitmore," I said to one of the girls who was busy organizing tools.

"Oh my God, we thought we were the only two girls here," She said pointing over to her co-worker who was heading to the breakfast line.

"Where are you guys from" I asked.

Mendocino, and you?

"Right here at Whitmore," I proudly replied. "Yeah, we didn't have to go very far, but since I was kicked out of my bed, I get to sleep on the lawn."

As we walked together to the breakfast line, I asked her what it was like to work for the Forest Service. During the course of the summer, I heard CDF crew members call the Forest Service the "Forest Circus." It was apparent that here was a rivalry between these two agencies. This girl firefighter told me, much to my shock, that they got to leave their station after hours if they wanted and they got paid overtime plus hazard pay when working on a fire. This bit of information threw me for a loop.

I was getting my whopping $550.00 a month and had worked days upon days with no time off and certainly no overtime pay. What the hell was that? I was getting a funny feeling that maybe I should had investigated this firefighting business a little further and checked out the Forest Service. She also told me that the Forest Service had been hiring women for a few years before CDF, but there still wasn't a lot of them.

The breakfast table was filled with pancakes, eggs, bacon, sausage, pastries, fresh fruit and French toast. This sure beat the hell out of those nasty C-rations! I filled my plate and pigged out with the Forest Service girls on the lawn in the shade. They told me about life at their station in Mendocino. Just like us at Whitmore, they worked on their trucks, kept the station clean, etc., but all in all, it seemed pretty kicked back there. I wondered if they had a better deal than what I got with CDF.

With full bellies, we rolled out our paper sleeping bags and tried to get some sleep. It was hot and I really had no use for this sleeping bag except to keep the bugs off. Shade was scarce and there were many fighting for the shady spots under the trees. I tried like hell to sleep but the constant sounds of yelling, helicopters, generators, trucks and radios made it impossible. Every half hour I woke up in the blaring sun and had to move once again to the shade. This went on until the late afternoon when I finally gave up and prepared for my night shift. As I headed toward my truck I heard a man say "excuse me, ma'am." I turned around to see a civilian with a note pad and camera walking towards me.

"I'm a reporter for the Redding Record Searchlight newspaper and I'd like to ask you a few questions if you have time."

"Sure," I said setting down my gear.

He asked my name, how long I'd been working for CDF, and how I liked working there. I was taken off-guard from being interviewed by a news reporter and I just blurted out, "I work with a great bunch of people." (partially true) "They treat me like and equal and don't try and make me feel bad by asking me to do something they know I can't do." I couldn't believe the complete bullshit that came out of my mouth. He closed his little book and told me that it would be in the next day's paper. Feeling like an instant celebrity, I picked up my gear and headed to another night out on the fire line.

**Shasta College Boxing Club
Three minutes at the bag**

Jan & Lauren front and center

Disbanded hockey players go cross country

By CELINE PEOPLES

Coach Gary Lewis wanted more than one woman on his cross country team at Shasta College, and now he has seven, compliments of the disbanded women's field hockey team.

When the women's field hockey team folded in October because there were not enough players, six of the girls decided to try their hand at running cross country.

Angie Miller has been with the team since September and competed with other colleges.

"She is an outstanding performer," said Lewis, "and a number one runner with the team."

Of the other six ladies, Heidi Rulofson has run track before and Janet Cornett is not eligible to compete until October 20, when she will be 18.

Cornett has been in shin splints and according to Lewis, "She has been a little hampered."

Tami Ewing is progressing well, but pulled a muscle in her thigh which has hampered her, also.

Carol Angelo, Sheri Pueblo and Eileen Finn are all inexperienced with run-ning cross country, but are progressing. "They seem like a really good group of girls," said Lewis.

Lewis has only worked with the ladies about two weeks. But he is looking for their qualities so he can train each on an individual basis, just as he would train a new man.

"I find out what their capabilities are, and go from there," said Lewis. Lewis has not been working them so hard that they do not enjoy the team. "They've never done this before, and it's something new to them. You want them to enjoy what they're doing," said Lewis.

Right now Lewis is trying to up their mileage and build up their endurance, but he believes the ladies contribute as much to the team as a whole as the men do.

Lewis believes that having ladies on the team is advantageous. "I'm a firm believer in women's rights to the same opportunities as men," said Lewis.

Even though the men only compete with men and the ladies only compete with ladies, Lewis does not look at it as separate teams.

"I don't look at it as being a men's and a women's team; it's just a team. We have to treat everybody as an individual," said Lewis.

And now the ladies have the opportunity to contribute even more as a team because this year is the first to offer an official state meet for women and the first conference to offer women's track and field in Northern California.

That's me at the end as usual.
All that running did pay off!

Fire Girl Jan

AKA

Little Prick

Don't mess with me
I have a switch blade!

The mean 4x4 brush truck

A day of work at Whitmore

The dreaded degreasing of the trucks
1978

Changing the flat while heading to the fire

Fire camp at
Whitmore

The barracks and dining building are barely visible
amidst all of the fire camp trailers.

Fire at Whitmo
A hot, dirty job

By GREG BLACKMAN

Fighting the Whitmore fire is hot, dry, dirty work, and after a 12-hour shift on the fireline a firefighter's reward is a paper sleeping bag and a piece of hard ground. Even for the weary, sleep does not come easy.

"I only slept a couple hours," Don Feser of the U.S. Forest Service's Texas Canyon Hot Shot crew said Thursday. "It's too hot and the shade keeps shifting."

Jeff Bailey of the Little Tujunga Hot Shots agreed: "Every few hours you have to move to another spot of shade."

Several hundred of the 500 people battling the blaze are spread out in the spotty shade on the lawn of the Whitmore Forest Fire Station. Some have rigged makeshift shelters of cardboard boxes.

Sleep seems to have caught a few; others struggle vainly and the few who have given up altogether play cards.

An occasional female firefighter

can be seen among the crews. They are still unusual enough to attract attention but women are more in evidence than they were just a few years ago. "You never used to see a woman in fire camp," explained one veteran.

For Jan Cornett, a Shasta College student and a summer employee of the California Department of Forestry, the experience has been positive.

"I work with a great bunch of people. They treat me as an equal but don't try to make me feel bad by asking me to do something they know I can't do," said the small brunette as she shouldered her pack and headed for another night on the fireline.

Wednesday night's shift was a tough one. Wind-whipped flames caused more than one crew to retreat to an open area and watch the flames go by.

"We were in a meadow near the camp and could see flames 350 degrees around us," said one hand crew member.

"It was just like the Fourth July," said another. "we could 200-foot flames and great showers sparks."

Medical personnel at the fire camp aid station treated nearly 100 people in the first 30 hours of operation, but most of the ailments called for little more than a Band-Aid or aspirin.

"But wait until the third day when people start getting tired and the poison oak hits," said one of the emergency medical technicians.

Surprisingly, there have been just five cases of heat exhaustion, despite the high temperatures.

Chris Fontana, who runs the portable weather station at the Whitmore fire camp, had good news for firefighters. Local temperature is going down. It had gone from the low hundreds Wednesday to the upper 90s Thursday and should drop again today.

Cooler temperatures and a few more shifts on the fireline, and make sleeping a lot ea

Southfork Lookout Tower 1978

View to the North

Very smoggy view to the east over the Redding Basin

Another motley bunch of men that I worked with on
a brush crew after CDF, but that's another story.
                                I finally got really good
                                       at swinging an axe

Osborne Firefinder

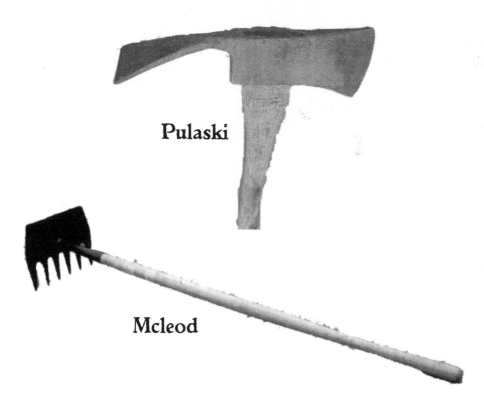

Pulaski

Mcleod

In 1978 CDF changed the name to California Department of Forestry. However, we were still issued the old patch that said Division of Forestry.

This is the actual patch I wore on my uniform.

Eleven
The Burn Over

On night number two of what was officially called the Whitmore Fire, the situation got worse since the outside temperature was still over 100 degrees, and the winds had been pretty strong. The fire experts hoped to have this fire contained in a day or so. This was wishful thinking and didn't happen. The fire swiftly moved into very thick timber and steep terrain and was only about 25 percent contained. Over 3000 acres of valuable forest had burned. Our crew traveled farther up the dusty dirt roads into the thick of things. The huge pine trees blew up like bombs and I tried to take some photos of this spectacle with my little instant camera. As I sat in the back of the truck, I couldn't help but watch this spectacular show of fire with awe and amazement. Fire was devastating and beautiful at the same time and this fireworks show of Mother Nature was awesome. It was actually kind of cool.

The ever so annoying busy work task master, Singer was behind the wheel of our truck when he yelled out of the window. "Cornett and Gomez, I want you two to grab some back pumps and hold this line and don't let any fire cross the road." Huh? Hold what line?

You mean these 200 foot trees? What the Hell was he talking about? I was at a loss. Gomez and I put on our heavy metal back pumps and were left standing in the road while Singer, Mathers and Stackmore took off in the truck.

"Where the hell are they going?" I yelled to Gomez.

"Hell if I know, you head that way and I'll go up the road the other way."

Gomez marched down the road with his back pump and disappeared into the dark. I stood on the side of the road all by myself with my back pump sitting heavy and uncomfortable on my shoulders while the fire burned about 200 yards away, moving parallel to the road.

This fire was huge and I was told to hold some mysterious line. Singer was crazy. If this fire decided to come my direction and jump the road, there was wasn't a damned thing that me with my little piss pump could do to stop it. They would find a pile of ashes (me) and my metal pack pump on top, a little sooty but for the most part intact. Standing along the road in bewilderment, I squirted water out of my back pump to put out little spot fires in the grass and pine needles around me. I walked up and down the road for about 45 minutes putting out little fires until I was completely out of water. Ok, this was insane; I had to go find Gomez and most of all our truck. I started walking the direction of where I last saw Gomez. It was smokier than before and I realized the wind shifted. The fire was moving towards me. Oh shit, now what the hell do I do? Run? Where the hell was the truck? Where the hell was Gomez? I was completely panicked and freaked out.

The trees were blowing up not far from me and the heat and smoke were unbearable. It was extremely hard to breath and I found myself holding my breath. The trees were crowning and it was just a matter of a few minutes that this fire would go over top of me and over the road. Hold the line my ass! Singer was crazy!

Mother Nature's fire works show wasn't so cool anymore. It was completely uncool! I needed to find some air so I could breathe. It was time to run. Through teary eyes, I spotted Gomez jogging towards me with the truck rolling up right behind him. Mathers was hanging out of the window yelling at us to jump on because we were getting the hell out of there. Thank the Lord! As the truck continued to roll, Gomez and I threw the pumps on the back and scrambled to our jump seats. Singer floored it as the fire began to jump the road right where I was standing moments before. Dust was boiling up behind us and we could barely see where we were going through the thick dense smoke that engulfed the entire area.

"What the hell was that all about?" I yelled to Gomez.

"Hell if I know, that scared the living shit out of me, that was a close one," replied Gomez. I was in bewilderment as to why we were left on the road with only back pumps in such a volatile situation.

We continued to drive aimlessly along the fire roads, kicking up more dust that settled into even more huge dirt clods up my nose. I could have planted tomatoes up there. Suddenly Singer hit the breaks and made a quick U-turn. We got a call on the radio to head back to the part of the fire that we had just left. I couldn't believe it. This had to be a bad joke on us! We were told that a bulldozer was sitting in the forest unmanned and we were to go protect it from being burned up.

As we traveled up a very remote fire road on our way to protect the dozer, the scene became a little spooky. The fire was very intense around us and we rolled over an immense amount of fire hose that was hastily left strewn all over the road by another fire crew. This couldn't be good. We kept going in. There was more and more hose left on the road. This was a huge warning and Singer wasn't seeing it. We needed to be going the other way!

We continued on. The fire was huge and all around us on both sides of the road. We finally arrived in a very small clearing to find a huge beast of a D-8 Caterpillar bulldozer. I assumed the driver must have taken off with the smart crews who left their hoses and escaped to a safer place. It finally became clear to Singer that we were ,screwed and that the fire was about to come down on us with a vengeance. The thousands of dollars worth of hose left in the road in a frenzied haste should have been Singer's first clue.

When we were rolling over the abandoned hose, he still had time to tell dispatch that the situation had deteriorated with no good outcome, so why didn't he? We were trapped with no way out. We had about three minutes to prepare for the fire that was imminently going to burn over us. We scrambled off the truck as he fired up the pump and yanked out the booster hose. We all quickly took turns hosing one another down with water until our Nomex suits were completely soaked through to our skin.

Mathers was up on top of the truck pulling out our MSA tanks; the breathing apparatus that was going to save us from dying of smoke inhalation. We were taught in fire class that a firefighter would most likely pass out from breathing the thick dense smoke before they burned to death. I scrambled to get the MSA mask on my face. My hands shook fiercely. I could barely hear Singer over the roar of the fire when he yelled for us to crouch down beside the truck as low as we could. I lay flat on the ground covering my head with my arms. It was very hot and the roar of the fire sounded like a locomotive coming through and we were on the tracks. The extremely hot wind hit my face, and the roar was deafening. Out of the corner of my eye, I saw a yellow figure running towards the bulldozer. Singer pulled off his mask and screamed "STAAACKMOOORE." Stackmore ditched his MSA and ran like a rabbit ignoring Singer's order to return. "STAAAACKMOORE." Singer's screams were faint above the roar of the oncoming apocalypse. Giving up, Singer put his mask back on and crouched beside me while Stackmore disappeared behind the bulldozer.

The fire crowned over top of us as the trees and brush blew up all around. I was burning alive. I thought I was a goner. This was it. I thought about my family and why the hell I signed up for this madness. I prayed for God to get me out of this mess. Panic set in and my breathing became fast and heavy inside my face mask. I felt my skin start to burn through my wet clothing and tears swelled in my eyes but this time it wasn't from the smoke, I was crying because I thought I was going to die. I didn't want to look around to see the show that I once thought was cool. I didn't like the show anymore nor did I think it was pretty. I knew that Stackmore was already dead, he had to be. The fire created a tornado-type wind and the sound seemed to get louder, if that was even possible. This was a holocaust and I was in the middle of it. The stinging, burning pain was so bad that I prayed for this ridiculous situation to end one way or the other.

Then in an instant it was over. The sound and wind died down and so did the heat. I lifted my head and looked around at the trees that still had a smattering of flames. The fire had burned over us and we were alive. Stackmore, where was Stackmore? I knew his charred body was just beyond the dozer. There was no way he could have survived this without his MSA. I took off my mask and heard familiar whimpering.

I ran over to the dozer found Stackmore underneath of it crying and sobbing. "Hey Stackmore, you ok?" I knelt next to him. Stackmore was clearly in shock and couldn't stop sobbing. Singer came over and helped Stackmore to his feet and took him back to the truck. He continued to cry and seemed to have completely lost his mind. This incident finally put him over the edge of no return. I felt sorry for him.

My arms hurt badly and I rolled up my sleeves to take a look. The skin was red and showed signs of blisters in some spots. I was amazed to have received such burns without my clothing catching fire; Nomex really worked. That heat was intense!

"Hey check this out," said Mathers pointing to the truck. The paint was blistered and the light on top was melted down to a big blob of plastic. The metal of the truck was too hot to touch. I looked over at the dozer and it looked the same as it did when we first arrived, not a scratch. My rage boiled as hot as the fire that melted the truck. I looked at Singer with disgust. He was hell bent on saving this big piece of shit dozer that would have never burned anyway and no doubt was insured. How was I going to survive the rest of this fire with Singer at the helm? I thought Stackmore was the one that was going to get me killed. Boy was I wrong! Singer was now the one that was scaring the shit out of me!

We solemnly loaded our blistered and burned bodies onto our blistered truck and left the dozer sitting exactly the way we found it. Stackmore sat across from me with his head in his hands. This time

Gomez didn't punch him in the arm as usual, but patted him on the back telling him it would be ok. I was chilled to the bone from my wet clothes and burned skin in the night air and I shook uncontrollably. We headed back down the road in complete silence once again crossing all of the abandoned fire hose. Seeing the hose, I just shook my head. That entire experience was so preventable. We could have died.

Safe at the fire station I got treated for my burns. Armed with some sort of burn cream, I immediately headed to the lawn to secure a piece of shade and struggled to sleep in the extreme heat on my paper sleeping bag. Sleep wasn't coming easily since I was constantly thinking of my close call with death not to mention my arms and legs hurt like hell. "Did you hear? Stackmore quit and left the party. Yep, the second we got back to the station, Stackmore packed his car and peeled out of the parking lot," Mathers said with a laugh. Poor Stackmore, he probably had to get some psychiatric counseling after that experience. I really felt sorry for him, but at least he wasn't our concern any longer.

Later that afternoon and after filling my stomach with a big fat juicy and much deserved steak, I once again loaded up my gear and headed back out for another night of adventure. "Will Singer get another chance to finally finish me off?" I thought solemnly as I marched over to the truck. I think the entire fire camp heard my sigh of relief when I saw Abbott behind the wheel of 2475 instead of Singer. I didn't have to work with Singer after this incident. I was very happy as I had a better chance of not dying after all!

This night we headed to a ranch situated a few miles from Whitmore that was in danger of going up in flames. We were told that the fire was approaching and that we were to stand by the structures with our trucks and hoses, just in case. I was a little suspicious since this is the same story we were told concerning the dozer! I surveyed the area and saw large lawns with green grass surrounding the buildings with a lot defensible space between the buildings and the big pines; we had a chance of saving this ranch. We parked our truck on one of the large lawns and waited. The flames were really kicking up all around the ranch, but so far the fire was keeping its distance from the valuable buildings. Gomez, Mathers and I dragged hose out of the truck and got ready. The pine trees became engulfed in flames close to the ranch and once again I felt that we were in another dangerous situation, but at least we had something very valuable to save, someone's home!

I hadn't had much sleep in the last three days, and I was getting dog tired, but the intense fire moving upon us gave me a spurt of energy. I kicked it up a notch and dragged hose with strength I didn't know I had. The fire burned around the compound of buildings and we were able to keep the fire at bay but for how much longer was the question. Another fire truck arrived and this one had Summit City emblazoned on the side. It was Chris! What were the odds? I was so happy to see him. It had only been three days since I left him in Summit city but it seemed like an eternity with everything that has happened to me.

Boy did I have a lot to tell him. He was shocked and pretty pissed off when I told him that Singer almost got us killed the night before, twice! I was so happy to be standing on this lawn with my hero and felt a sense of security that everything would be alright. With the help of one more truck, we were able to save the structures and the fire moved on and past the ranch. When things were under control around the ranch, Abbott told us to load up; we were moving on. With a heavy heart, I said goodbye to Chris and we headed down the road.

During the night we spent time moving down fire roads and putting out hot spots that threatened to kick back up. Abbott seemed to know what he was doing and we actually got things accomplished. The night was long and I was extremely tired. At 3 a.m. I broke out my C-rations and dug out the cookies and chocolate. We were a man short without Stackmore, but I didn't miss him. He never did much anyway and was mostly in the way. I hoped he found something that he could do with his life.

Towards the end of our shift, Abbott gave us the order to roll up hose and get ready to head out. I dutifully started picking up the hose as instructed when without warning it became pressurized in my hands and my thumb got caught in a kink. I frantically tried to wrench my thumb free and in a panic I gave it a good yank. My glove flew off and blood was everywhere. Was my thumb still there? I didn't want to know and I couldn't look.

Blood dripped down my arm as I held up my hand. Abbott took one look and said "Oh God, I'm so sorry; I accidentally charged the wrong hose."

"Why were you charging any hose? You just told us to roll them up," I shrieked.

Thinking that my thumb was gone, I felt dizzy. "Is my thumb still there?" I asked as I went down on my knees. Abbott took me by the arm and led me over to a county fire engine crew. Unlike CDF'rs who weren't trained to even apply Band-aids, the county and local fire crews were Emergency Medical Technicians and Paramedics or were at least trained in basic first aid. They had all sorts of medical equipment on their trucks. "How bad is it?" I held my thumb out for the EMT to take a look. "We'll it's on there, but you'll need some stitches. It's pretty deep." He wrapped my thumb with thick gauze and I started to feel dizzy again. "Ok, come over here and sit down and put your head between your knees," said the fireman.

"You're back," said the fire camp nurse as she unwrapped my thumb and washed away the blood. It hurt like hell when she scrubbed and stitched the wound – the dizziness returned. I looked like a deranged hitchhiker as I walked back to my truck with a cartoon looking bandage on my thumb. Since I was on the injured list and not able to return to the fire line, I was given a new assignment as Captain Harris's driver. Wow, driver, this sounded really easy and fun! I really didn't understand why Harris couldn't drive himself, but they had to give me something to do! How hard could this new job be?

TWELVE
Wild Rides & Night Hike

As my new job of the Captain's driver, I was to report to a large open field where a makeshift helicopter landing spot was established. Harris waved me over to a large helicopter with the rotors turning. "Hop in," he said. The helicopter was huge and filled with fire bosses. Harris sat next to me and in an instant, we shot straight up in the air then forward like a bullet. My stomach was still on the ground, however, and I felt a bit queasy. We pitched and turned with great speed through the mountains and dipped into the canyons and along the ridges. I could clearly see where the Whitmore fire had burned and where it was headed. I felt a tap on my shoulder and turned to see Harris frantically pointing to something out of the window. I looked down and saw a tiny clearing with a bulldozer sitting in the middle.

The area around the clearing was completely charred with not a living thing left. "Stackmore's Clearing," Harris yelled in my ear with a big grin on his face. I looked down again at the clearing and wondered how we had made it out of there alive. The fire had burned well beyond the clearing and moved up the side of another ridge. Our helicopter flew in and around the huge columns of smoke as the fire bosses conversed and looked at maps of the area. My stomach gave me fits and I was thankful when we finally landed with my breakfast safely intact.

Back at the station, Captain Harris interrogated me about the burn over incident in the clearing. He told me that there would be an investigation on the incident along with some sort of recourse. I had my doubts about that, but he seemed sincere. Harris was a really nice jovial man and I thought I would like driving him around. I got behind the wheel of our International Scout and my first assignment was to drive him to the grocery store to get some items for his wife. She must have been beside herself with all the commotion and noise going on right outside her house at the once sleepy little fire station. With groceries delivered, we headed up the mountain to do some surveying. It was getting dark and Harris had to use the flashlight to see his topography maps. Just before we started to climb a pretty big hill, I put the Scout into four-wheel drive by getting out and locking up the front hubs. The dust on the road had turned into a deep powder and I sank up to my ankles.

As we drove along the fire roads, I listened with interest as Harris told me all sorts of his personal fire stories from a career that spanned 20 years. "I knew that one day we'd have a girl come to Whitmore," he said. "But I never knew how I'd feel about it until you showed up. You're an alright kid in my book and you really try hard." I smiled and felt pretty darned proud to be the captain's driver. I wondered what my crew was doing on the fire line. Maybe we would run into them, I hoped so! The dust was getting deeper and it was hard to get the little Scout to move. In the darkness and the thick clouds of dust that we stirred up, I could barely make out the road in front of us. Harris studied the map and said that a left turn was coming up. I took the left turn and all of a sudden the Scout wouldn't move any further. I gave it some gas and the wheels spun deeper in the dust. "Ok, let's see what's going on." Harris got out of the Scout to survey the situation. My dust covered watch said that it was 11.30 p.m. "Let's put some wood under the tires for traction," said Harris as he headed out into the darkness. We searched the immediate area for small pieces of wood but most of the pieces were huge and required a chainsaw. The only tool we had in the Scout was a shovel. We were screwed.

I got back into the Scout, trying once again to drive out of the deep dust. As Harris pushed, I gave it the gas. The tires dug in deeper and were barely visible. We were stranded in the middle of the woods, several miles away from the station. Harris got on the radio and called for help but was informed that rescue wouldn't be for a few hours. We were told that a hotshot crew was just up the road a few miles and they could possibly help push the Scout. Harris handed me the flashlight and said "Get to walking."

"By myself?" I looked at him in bewilderment.

"I have to stay here with the truck in case someone decides to come up and rescue us. In the mean time, see if you can find that Hot Shot crew."

With nothing but a flashlight, no radio, and certainly no firefighting equipment, I started walking up the dark dusty road into an abyss of dense forest. The headlights of the Scout no longer offered any assistance and I could only see what was in the very small beam of my flashlight. There were all sorts of strange noises coming from the forest. Wild animals? My vivid imagination? I heard stories that there were bears and mountain lions in these woods. It felt like wild, hungry eyes were watching me and it gave me the creeps.

After about an hour of walking I got the feeling that the hotshot crew had moved on. I couldn't decide if I should keep walking to oblivion or go back to the Scout. I kept walking. I came upon a fork in the road. Crap! I stood there and pondered for a minute when my gut said to take the left fork, it looked more traveled. I couldn't believe that Harris sent me out on a wild goose chase in the middle of the night by myself. I kept walking. After another hour of brisk walking, I finally saw something up ahead. People? Oh My God, it was people! It was the hotshot crew sleeping in their paper sleeping bags. "Hey!" I jogged up to the closest person. "My captain and I are stuck down the road about six miles that way." Can you guys come and help us?"

The sleepy hotshot crew member stared at me with a blank expression. He must have been startled to see a little girl come out of the woods wearing what seemed to be firefighting clothing. "Where in the living hell did you come from?" He said as he looked past me down the road.

"I've been hiking for the past two hours trying to get help."

"Well holy shit," he said. The other hotshot guys were all up and had me circled. They couldn't believe that I hiked up there by myself with only a flashlight.

"We can't go back down the mountain; we are about to head out to another area. But, there is a D-8 Cat just up the road a ways, really close. He's sitting up on top of that ridge about a half mile off the road. He may be able to help you."

"Ok, I'll keep hiking," I said with disappointment. With my flashlight starting to die, I left the hotshot crew behind and marched on looking for the dozer.

The beam of my flashlight was very dim and I had a hard time seeing where I was going. I came upon a swath of dirt veering off of the road that was obviously cut by a dozer so I followed it. The going was tough and slow as I trudged along in the deep thick dust. As I followed the tracks, I decided that if I couldn't find the dozer, I'd just hightail it back to the hotshot crew and join up with them. The hill was steep and I huffed and puffed as I climbed. Finally reaching the top, I found no dozer. OK, hotshot crew get ready for a new member. Just as I turned to go back down the hill I caught a glimpse of yellow just behind a grove of trees on the other side of the ridge. It was the dozer! I was so relieved to see a person sitting at the controls.

The startled dozer operator's eyes got wide when he saw me coming towards him. I had to climb up to the cab of this giant machine which seemed to be 20 feet from the ground. Before he could get a word out, I rattled the entire story of my night hike in the forest and the stuck Scout. "Ok, well then hang on and I'll take you back." The cab of the dozer only had one seat for the operator and there was no room to stand inside so I clung onto the roll cage on the out side of the cab like a little monkey. I found it difficult to find a place to put my feet so I had to kind of straddle with one foot inside the door of the cab with the other outside.

With the huge bandage on my thumb, I had a hard time getting a good grip so I wrapped both arms around one of the bars of the roll cage. If I fell off, I would have been crushed into the ground like a bug. "You on good?" asks the driver. "I think so," I said. He flipped a switch and big spotlights came on that lit up the hillside. He then started the engine of this monster which made it vibrate profusely. We hadn't even moved yet, and I was having a hard time keeping my feet in place. Then with a huge jerk, we lurched forward and immediately started to climb over the ridge.

We crawled along slowly as the tracks (these are the wheels just like what are on a military tank) tore up the earth beneath us. The driver yelled "Hang on!" as the engine revved louder and the dozer moved up and over the ridge. We crawled along the hillside completely tilted and I hung on for dear life, sideways. Now we were going straight down the hill. This ride was more of a thrill than anything I'd ridden at the fair. I scrambled to regain my footing as we jetted straight down off of the ridge and became sideways again. I gritted my teeth and my arms hurt because I had them wrapped so tight around the roll bar.

Up, down sideways, the engine revved as we continued to crawl off of the mountain tearing down big bushes and small sapling trees in our path. My nerves were completely shot when we finally reached the road and flat ground. "How was that?" he said with a grin. "Holy cow, that was better than the Tilt-a-Whirl, but I gotta say that going sideways part really scared the living hell out of me," I said laughing. He put the dozer back in gear and we crawled along the road to rescue my Captain and the Scout. As we passed the hotshot crew, they all lined the road and waved to the little girl spectacle clinging for life on the side of the dozer. I was too afraid to let go so I just give them all a nod and smile. Dozers don't move very fast so it was a painfully long ride back. It was almost 4 a.m. when we found Harris sitting in the passenger seat of the Scout with a big smile on his face. "I knew you'd do it Cornett, but I never expected a dozer, well done!"

THIRTEEN
After the Fire

Wurphen we finally rolled into the station the sun was up and I looked like Pig Pen from the Peanuts cartoons. After spending all night walking in ankle deep dust and the crazy ride on the dozer, dirt was flying off of me with every step I took. Just as I finished up with my breakfast on the big lawn a woman walked up to me. "Hi Jan, I have a surprise for you." It was captain Harris's wife and she motioned for me to come with her into her home. I'd been at Whitmore all summer, mowing and weeding all around this house, but I had never been inside. "You want to jump in my bathtub and get some of that dirt out?" she asked. I was stunned. "Come on, it'll be our little secret. I know what you've been through this past week with the burn over and your hike last night."

The inside of the Captains house was nice and I dared not get near the furniture since I was so filthy. In a flash, Mrs. Harris returned with a robe, towel a bottle of shampoo and bubble bath. Bubble bath! I almost cried. As I ran the bath, I dutifully handed her my grimy clothes that I had been wearing for a week and she tossed them in the washer. I filled the bathtub to the brim with bubbles. There was so much dirt that I had to drain the water twice so I could wash my mud filled hair. I had so much dirt and soot on me that I might have clogged her plumbing. After two glorious hours of soaking and scrubbing, I came out of the bathroom a new person, almost human. She handed me an ice tea and we sat in her glorious air conditioned living room and chatted while my clothes dried. She listened intently while I told her my adventures of the summer. I knew from that day on that I would never forget her kindness as long as I lived. After two more days of driving Captain Harris and a couple more helicopter rides, which my stomach never got used to, I was taken off of the injured list and returned to my truck. Abbott was still our engineer and I hadn't seen Singer in a few days. I wondered where they were hiding him.

Crews were getting the Whitmore fire under control and after 26 straight days of over 100 degree temperatures, the weather finally started to get a little cooler. I was still on the night crew and it felt good to be back on good ole 2475. With the fire almost contained, most of the crews were packing up and leaving Whitmore. At the peak of the fire, there were over 1200 firefighters with scores of fire trucks, bulldozers and other equipment encamped at our little station. With things settling down, only a couple hundred firefighters remained. "Cornett, get the truck and bring it out front," said Abbott as he handed me the keys. Holy crap, I get to drive the truck? The fire truck? The most I ever got to drive the truck was backing it into the garage. I learned how to use the mirrors and squeezed it into the bay perfectly every time. This time I got to actually drive it forward and all the way to the front of the station. I ran to the garage with keys in hand and eagerly got behind the wheel. Since I was pretty short, I had to stretch my neck to see over the large steering wheel. I expected to see Abbott and the rest of the guys waiting for me out front, but they were nowhere to be found. Parking in front of the station as instructed, I took the keys out of the ignition (mistake number 1) and got out. My bootlace was untied, so I set the keys on top of a tall brick fence post (mistake number 2) and bent down to tie my laces. When I was done, I reached for the keys and all I felt was the brick of the post. No keys! My heart pounded as I got up on top of the fence rail to search for the keys. To my horror there was a huge hole at the top of the brick fence post. The hole ran the length of the post all the way to the ground, about four feet. I lost the truck keys down this dark hole.

Mathers walked up and saw me peering down the post. "I lost the keys to the truck," I said weakly. "Oh shit, Little Prick, you did it now." We both stood there looking down the hole. "Don't we have a spare set?" I asked. "Harris has em locked in the office and he's not here. We gotta fish these out." Mathers got a flashlight out of the truck and shot the beam down the hole. "I see em," he said. "See if you can find a wire coat hanger." I sprinted to the barracks blowing by Abbott who looked at me curiously. I came out with a hanger to find Abbott, Gomez and Mathers all peering down the hole with the flashlight. I looked down at my boots feeling like a complete idiot. Mathers made a hook with the coat hanger and tried to fish out the keys. "It ain't long enough, get me another one." Once again, I sprinted to the barracks. This time he hooked the two coat hangers together and worked feverishly to fish out the keys. It was getting late and we were supposed to already be heading up the mountain. I felt sick, I was so embarrassed. "Got em," he said as he slowly pulled the wire from the hole with the truck keys hanging off the end. "Don't ever give the keys to Little Prick again," he said. I had to agree with him. I finally got my chance to drive the truck and I managed to lose the keys within minutes.

As we rode back up to the fire line, I looked up at the melted light bar on our truck and flashed back to the dreadful night of the burn-over. We were damned lucky. Since the fire was almost under control, we were mostly putting out small hot spots that were still glowing here and there along the mountain sides. Although the weather was a little cooler, in the mid 90s, it was still hot and miserable on the dusty red clay roads.

Eventually all of the outside fire crews left, and Whitmore was once again quiet with just our little group remaining. We got to move back to our barracks and we were back to cooking our own food. It was nice and quiet since Stackmore was no longer with us and we didn't have to put up with any scratching and snoring. Whitmore was back to normal but with that normalcy came the return of Singer. Once we were pretty much done with the mop-up of the Whitmore fire, we went back to the daily grind and Singer's busy work.

With fire season winding down, I was changing my mind about going back to school. Giving myself that option, I had to quit in time to enroll for classes and my employment as a firefighter ended.

During the 1978 fire season, the Whitmore crew responded to a total of 45 dispatches, not including the calls we took on our little fire tour.

"Gonna miss you Little Prick, you signing up next year?" Mathers asked as I packed up my car to leave Whitmore forever.

"I really don't know Mathers, this was quite an experience, but I don't know if I want to do it again."

I felt a sharp punch to the arm. It was Compton standing there with his usual smirk. "If I have to work with a girl next year, I guess I'll let you come back Little Prick." I punched him back and told him to eat shit. I felt honored!

Driving away from Whitmore through the tall Ponderosa pines that lined the road, I felt a little more grown up. I had no idea what I would do with my life when I returned to the civilian world. I learned how to do some very hard work and pushed myself beyond my limits as a female. Did females really have limits? I didn't believe so at the time and still don't. Yes, I had my challenges dealing with the physical aspects of the job since I was so small. I was also young, inexperienced in life, and had to deal with the issue of not being accepted by some of the crew. I tried to push myself beyond those challenges. I also learned at a young age about mortality, especially my own. Life is short so live every day like it's your last. Being one of the first women firefighters for CDF is something that I'm very proud of and I'm glad I decided to take the scary plunge into the unknown. Because of my short adventure as a fire girl, I proved to myself that I could do anything that I put my mind to. I never stopped trying new and exciting things in my life and will continue to blaze new trails and encourage others to do the same.

"Only those who risk of going too far can possibly find out how far they can go."

T.S. Eliot

Epilogue

After my stint with CDF as a seasonal firefighter, I made the final decision not to immediately go back to school. I moved in with Chris and we lived together for a couple of years. I ended up going back to work for the California Department of Forestry, but not as a firefighter, I was on a brush crew where I worked the next winter freezing my ass off cutting brush and falling trees; still using only hand tools. I ended up being pretty handy with an axe and a brush hook; Compton would have been proud. I eventually became a volunteer firefighter for the Summit City Fire Department and learned a few more firefighting skills. However, I still never learned first aid, so on medical calls, I drove the squad and took down patient information. As a matter of fact, I realized that I don't do well with blood and gore so being a first responder just wasn't in the cards for me. I eventually fulfilled my dream of becoming a professional musician performing around the country.

Operations at CDF have certainly changed from what they were 30 years ago. For instance, long gone are the days of a weeklong crash courses on wildland firefighting with no first aid training. Over the years, the California Department of Forestry changed its operations (now called Cal Fire) and became the State's fire department. Cal Fire not only responds to wildland fires, they are the first responders in structure fires, auto crashes, rescues and hazmat emergencies. Since the position of seasonal firefighter is extremely competitive, Cal Fire advises their prospective employees to already have an Emergency Medical Technician Certificate, their fire science classes under their belts as well as the completion of the 67 hour wildland fire academy. Back in the olden days, we didn't have fire shelters, personal radios and didn't get much training. Firefighters today carry all sorts of life saving equipment including fire shelters that they can deploy in case of a burn over. Each firefighter also carries a radio with extra batteries and their goggles and clothing have improved over the years which offer much better protection.

With the arrival of technology such as satellites, cell phones and improved aircraft, many of the lookout towers in California were put out of commission. Over the years, the number of active CDF and Forest Service lookout towers decreased dramatically from several hundred to approximately 90 active Forest Service or CDF manned towers. Most of the towers, such as Southfork Lookout, were demolished while some towers with the huts still intact are rented out to hikers.

There are many more women firefighters today but they are still in the minority and only make up about five percent of the entire Cal Fire firefighting force. Some of the pioneer women firefighters from the early days stayed on and moved up the ranks and eventually retired as high ranking fire officials.

I could have very well been the first female firefighter to be killed in a burn over in 1978 but by the grace of God, I wasn't. It wasn't until 2004 when 23 year old Eva Schicke from the CDF Columbia California Helitack Crew was the first CDF female firefighter to be killed in the line of duty. Notes from the official CDF report explained that her crew had to take emergency action on a fire in the Stanislaus National Forest near Groveland when without any warning, a sudden wind shift and fire flare up overran their position. The flare up and

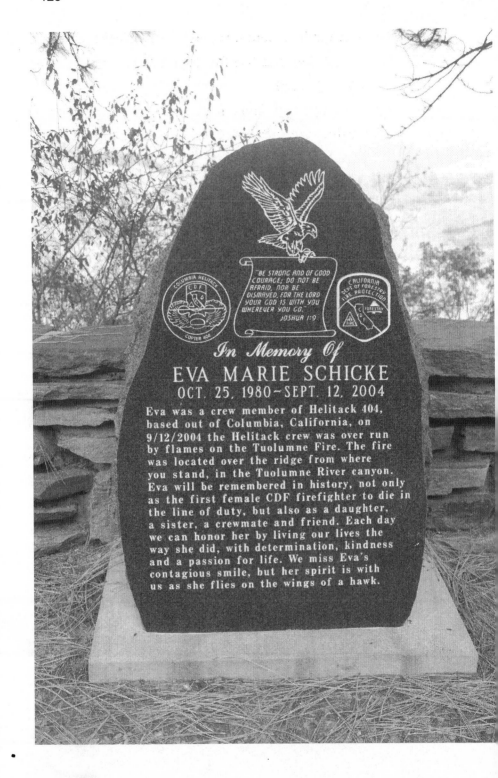

"BE STRONG AND OF GOOD COURAGE; DO NOT BE AFRAID, NOR BE DISMAYED, FOR THE LORD YOUR GOD IS WITH YOU WHEREVER YOU GO."
JOSHUA 1:9

In Memory Of

EVA MARIE SCHICKE

OCT. 25, 1980 – SEPT. 12, 2004

Eva was a crew member of Helitack 404, based out of Columbia, California, on 9/12/2004 the Helitack crew was over run by flames on the Tuolumne Fire. The fire was located over the ridge from where you stand, in the Tuolumne River canyon. Eva will be remembered in history, not only as the first female CDF firefighter to die in the line of duty, but also as a daughter, a sister, a crewmate and friend. Each day we can honor her by living our lives the way she did, with determination, kindness and a passion for life. We miss Eva's contagious smile, but her spirit is with us as she flies on the wings of a hawk.

burn over happened in 30 seconds. While the rest of the crew made it to their safety zones Eva was five feet from her safety zone when she was overtaken by the fire.

Wildland firefighting is dangerous business. This book is dedicated to all of the brave men and women who risk their lives and some who gave the ultimate sacrifice to serve to protect our planet from devastating fire.

I want to thank my good friend Chuck Vanevenhoven who is a retired fire Chief for Sutter County in Northern California with a fire service career that spanned 34 years. Chuck started his fire career with CDF in the early 70s and told me they didn't even wear Nomex back then, just long sleeve shirts. Chuck gave me the inspiration to write this book and he was my "go-to" technical adviser regarding things that I had long forgotten.

He also shared with me these traditional firefighter sayings.

"Teann cach abhaile" (Celtic/Gaelic) Motto often used in the traditional fire service meaning – "everyone goes home."

"A Good Jake" A traditional term meaning a good firefighter; someone you want on your crew.

P.S. For my fellow crew members that were hard on me- THANK YOU! You made me tough as nails. I'm forever grateful for the opportunity to work with each of you. I learned a lot about myself that summer!

Love Little Prick

Acknowledgments

This project took me a full year in research and writing. I had to submit public records requests to a few state agencies and painfully waited for responses. I also had to dig through the recesses of my brain which hurt a bit too. I did have a little help though!

My husband and best friend Alex for always believing in me.
I love you.

William Gutierrez for once again being a great and honest editor of my work. I know the first draft was painful for you.
Fire fighter or Firefighter, I just couldn't decide!

Jen Belitz for sharing your photos and writing that wonderful foreword. You are one heck of a daredevil!

Chris W. for filling in a few of the gaps! Thank you for finding me, your timing was uncanny! Congratulations on 40 years of dedicated fire service (Retired 2014)

The California Department of Forestry webmaster for providing me with the much needed history of CDF women firefighters.

100% of the proceeds of Fire Girl are donated to the
Wildland Firefighter Foundation

Publisher's Note:
All of the images in the book plus bonus images can be seen in better quality and in full color at www.wildlandfirewomen.com.

Jan Mendoza lives with her husband Alex on a small ranch in Northern California. They have horses, dogs, a donkey and two house poodles that keep them extremely busy.

Jan is a speaker, life and business consultant, professional horse trick riding instructor, and a professional musician who writes her own songs and produces and films music videos. She is also retired from the State of California where she was a media spokesperson for four California State Agencies.

You can find more about Jan at www.janmendoza.com

49500274R00084

Made in the USA
Middletown, DE
17 October 2017